Teen Pregnancy and Lone Parents

ISSUES

Volume 133

Series Editor

Lisa Firth

Independence

First published by Independence
PO Box 295
Cambridge CB1 3XP
England

© Independence 2007

British Library Cataloguing in Publication Data
Teen Pregnancy and Lone Parents – (Issues Series)
I. Firth, Lisa II. Series
306.8'56'0941

ISBN 978 1 86168 379 3

Printed in Great Britain
MWL Print Group Ltd

Cover
The illustration on the front cover is by
Don Hatcher.

CONTENTS

Introduction

Teen Pregnancy and Lone Parents is the one hundred and thirty-third volume in the **Issues** series. The aim of this series is to offer up-to-date information about important issues in our world.

Teen Pregnancy and Lone Parents looks at teenage parents in the UK and at lone-parent families.

The information comes from a wide variety of sources and includes:
Government reports and statistics
Newspaper reports and features
Magazine articles and surveys
Website material
Literature from lobby groups
and charitable organisations.

It is hoped that, as you read about the many aspects of the issues explored in this book, you will critically evaluate the information presented. It is important that you decide whether you are being presented with facts or opinions. Does the writer give a biased or an unbiased report? If an opinion is being expressed, do you agree with the writer?

Teen Pregnancy and Lone Parents offers a useful starting-point for those who need convenient access to information about the many issues involved. However, it is only a starting-point. Following each article is a URL to the relevant organisation's website, which you may wish to visit for further information.

* * * * *

Teenagers: sexual health and behaviour

An overview

This article aims to provide key data about the sexual health and behaviour of teenagers throughout the United Kingdom (UK). Where possible, data is presented separately for England, Wales, Scotland and Northern Ireland. Please note that this data is not always directly comparable due to differences in methods of data collection and analysis between countries.

Where Great Britain is referred to, this covers England, Wales and Scotland.

Age of consent

⇨ In England and Wales, the age of consent to any form of sexual activity is 16 for both men and women, whether they are heterosexual, homosexual or bisexual.[1]

⇨ In Scotland, the age of heterosexual consent for women and for sex between men is 16.[2]

⇨ In Northern Ireland, the age of heterosexual consent for women and for sex between men is 17.[3]

⇨ Although there is no specific age of consent for lesbian sex laid down in statute in Scotland and Northern Ireland, a girl under 16 is not deemed capable of consenting to any sexual behaviour which could be deemed as sexual assault.

Sexual behaviour

The second National Survey of Sexual Attitudes and Lifestyles (Natsal 2000), which included over 11,000 men and women aged 16-44 in Great Britain,[4] found that:

⇨ the average age at first heterosexual intercourse was 16 for both men and women.

putting sexual health on the agenda

⇨ nearly a third of men and a quarter of women aged 16-19 had heterosexual intercourse before they were 16.

⇨ about 80% of young people aged 16-24 said that they had used a condom when they first had sex.

⇨ less than one in ten had used no contraception at all when they first had sex.

⇨ one in five young men and nearly half of young women aged 16-24 said they wished they had waited longer to start having sex. They were twice as likely to say this if they had been under 15 when they first had sex.

⇨ both young men and women aged 16-24 had had an average of three heterosexual partners in their lifetime.[5]

⇨ about 1% (0.9% men, 1.6% women) of 16-24-year-olds had had one or more new same sex partners in the previous year.[5]

Natsal 2000 did not include Northern Ireland. A separate survey carried out in 2000 by fpa in Northern Ireland and the University of Ulster included over 1,000 young people aged 14-25.[6] It found that:

⇨ the average age at first heterosexual intercourse was 15.6 years (14.9 for men and 15.9 for women).

⇨ just over a third had experienced sexual intercourse before 17 (the legal age of consent in Northern Ireland) and a quarter had sex before 16.

⇨ nearly two-thirds (63.8%) had used a condom when they first had sex, either alone or with another method of contraception.

- about a quarter had used no contraception at all when they first had sex.
- just under a third (31.6%) said they felt they had sex too early, and this was more likely (43%) if they had been under 16 at the time.
- on average, the sexually active 14-25-year-olds had had six sexual partners; the average for young women was five, and young men eight.

The sixth annual Gay Men's Sex Survey in 2002[7] included over 16,000 gay and other homosexually active men in the UK. The age range of respondents was 14-83; half were aged 25-39.

- The average age at which men first had any sexual experience with another man was 17.5 years.
- Of those who had engaged in anal intercourse (AI), the average age for first doing so was 20.6 years and 60% had used a condom.
- The first AI partner was, on average, about four years older.
- Men under 20 were significantly more likely to have had both male and female partners (11.3%) than men in other age groups (6.4%-7.9%). In a separate survey of lesbian and bisexual women,[8] the under-20s were more likely to have had sex with both men and women (24%).

Use of contraception

An Office for National Statistics survey[9] of women aged 16-49 in Great Britain found that:

- 57% of women aged 16-17 years old said they used contraception. The most common reason given for not using a method was that they were not in a sexual relationship.
- 39% of 16-17-year-olds said they used the pill and 33% condoms (some will use both).
- 86% of women aged 16-17 had heard of hormonal emergency contraception (EC).
- 10% of women aged 16-17 and 26% of women aged 18-19 had used EC at least once in the previous 12 months.

There is no equivalent survey data on contraceptive usage by teenagers in Northern Ireland. The following statistics relate only to women attending community family planning clinics in 2003-04.[10]

- 49% of women aged 16-19 were using the pill and 21% the condom as their main method of contraception.

82,000 women aged under 16 attended family planning clinics in England in 2004-05, over 8% of the resident female population

---

- Although women under 20 accounted for 31% of all EC provided through family planning clinics in Northern Ireland, only 4% of the overall total was those aged under 16.

Use of family planning services

- 82,000 women aged under 16 attended family planning clinics in England in 2004-05, over 8% of the resident female population. This has increased from nearly 5% in 1993-94.[11]
- 267,000 or 21% of the resident female population in England aged 16-19 years of age visited a family planning clinic in 2004-05. The percentage attending has remained steady since 1996-97.[11]

Teenage pregnancy

- The UK has the highest teenage birth and abortion rates in Western Europe.[12]

England[13]

In 2004, there were:

- 39,545 under-18 conceptions, a rate of 41.5 per 1,000 females aged 15-17. Nearly half (46%) of the pregnancies were terminated.
- 7,189 under-16 conceptions, a rate of 7.5 per 1,000 females aged 13-15. Over half (57.6%) of the pregnancies were terminated.

Wales[14]

In 2004, there were:

- 2,605 under-18 conceptions, a rate of 45.1 per 1,000 females aged 15-17. Just over a third (38.5%) of the pregnancies were terminated.
- 434 under-16 conceptions, a rate of 7.5 per 1,000 females aged 13-15. Nearly half (49.3%) of the pregnancies were terminated.

Scotland

(Unlike England and Wales, Scottish conception data includes miscarriages managed in hospitals as well as registered births and abortions.)[15]

In 2003-04, there were:

- 8,616 conceptions in 16-19-year-olds, a rate of 68.2 per 1,000 females in that age group. About 42% of the pregnancies were terminated.
- 706 under-16 conceptions, a rate of 7.5 per 1,000 13-15-year-olds. Over half (58.3%) of the pregnancies were terminated.

Northern Ireland

- Conception data is not available for Northern Ireland, due to the lack of complete data on the number of women having abortions. Abortion is only legal in Northern Ireland in exceptional circumstances.
- In 2005, 206 teenagers travelled to England to have an abortion,[16] although this number is likely to be an underestimate.
- In 2004, there were 1,486 teenage births (under 20), 2.3% of 15-19-year-olds.[17]

Abortion

England and Wales[16]

- In 2005, 18,230 women aged under 18 had an abortion. Of these, 3,786 were under 16.
- The under-18 abortion rate was 17.8 per 1,000 and the under-16 rate was 3.7.

Scotland[18]

- In 2005, 2,963 women aged 16-19 and 341 under-16s had an abortion.
- The abortion rate in 16-19-year-olds was 23.1 per 1,000.

Northern Ireland

(See Teenage pregnancy section.)

Sexually transmitted infections[19]

- The total number of new episodes of selected STIs in men and women aged 16-19 years seen at genitourinary medicine (GUM) clinics in the UK rose from 39,500 in 2001 to 51,810 in 2005, an increase of 31%.

⇨ In 2005, the highest rates of diagnoses among young people aged 16-19 were for chlamydia, genital warts and gonorrhoea.

⇨ Rates were higher among women than men in this age group.

⇨ Rates of diagnoses among women aged 16-19 were: chlamydia (1,377 per 100,000), genital warts (739 per 100,000) and gonorrhoea (136 per 100,000).

⇨ Rates of diagnoses among men aged 16-19 were chlamydia (510 per 100,000), genital warts (280 per 100,000), and gonorrhoea (102 per 100,000).

⇨ Results from the National Chlamydia Screening Programme in England[20] in 2004-05 showed that 11% of men and 13% of women aged 16-19 tested positive for chlamydia.

Knowledge of STIs

In an Office for National Statistics survey of over 7,000 adults in Great Britain:[9]

⇨ 85% of men and 93% of women aged 16-19 years knew that chlamydia is an STI.

However, of those respondents who recognised chlamydia as an STI:

⇨ 41% of men and 21% of women aged 16-19 years old didn't know that it doesn't always cause symptoms.

⇨ 57% of men and 32% of women aged 16-19 years old didn't know that it is easily treated by antibiotics.

In a survey of over 620,000 school children across the UK:[21]

⇨ 6% of male and female pupils aged 14-15 years old thought that HIV/AIDS can be treated or cured, whilst 17% thought that chlamydia can be treated or cured.

References

1 Sexual Offences Act 2003.
2 Sexual Offences (Scotland) Act 1976; Sexual Offences Amendment Act 2000.
3 Criminal Law Amendment (Northern Ireland) Act 1885; Children and Young Person's Act 1950; Sexual Offences Amendment Act 2000.
4 Wellings K et al, 'Sexual behaviour in Britain: early heterosexual experience', *Lancet*, vol 358, (2001), 1843-1850.
5 Johnson A et al, 'Sexual behaviour in Britain: partnerships, practices and HIV risk behaviours', *Lancet*, vol 358, (2001), 1835-1842.
6 Schubotz D et al, *Towards Better Sexual Health: A survey of sexual attitudes and lifestyles of young people in Northern Ireland. Research report* (London: **fpa**, 2003).
7 Hickson F et al, *Out and About. Findings from the United Kingdom Gay Men's Sex Survey 2002* (London: Sigma Research, 2003).

8 Henderson L et al, *First, Service. Relationships, sex and health among lesbian and bisexual women* (London: Sigma Research, 2002).
9 Rickards L et al, *Living in Britain: Results from the 2002 General Household Survey* (London: TSO, 2004). <http://www.statistics.gov.uk>
10 **fpa**, *Family Planning Services in Northern Ireland* (Belfast: **fpa**, 2004).
11 Department of Health, *NHS Contraceptive Services. England: 2004-05* (London: DH, 2005). <http://www.dh.gov.uk>
12 UNICEF, *A League Table of Teenage Births in Rich Nations* (Florence: Innocenti Research Centre, 2001).
13 Teenage Pregnancy Unit, *Teenage Conceptions for England 1998-2004.* <http://www.dfes.gov.uk>
14 Office for National Statistics, Unpublished data.
15 ISD Scotland, *Teenage Pregnancy.* <http://www.isdscotland.org>
16 Department of Health, *Abortion Statistics, England and Wales: 2005* (London: DH, 2005). Statistical Bulletin 2006/01. <http://www.dh.gov.uk>
17 **fpa**, *Teenage Pregnancy* (Belfast: **fpa**, 2005).
18 ISD Scotland, *Abortion.* <http://www.isdscotland.org>
19 Health Protection Agency, *Diagnoses and Rates of Selected STIs Seen at GUM Clinics, United Kingdom: 2001-2005* (London: HPA, 2006). <http://www.hpa.org.uk>
20 National Chlamydia Screening Programme, *Looking Back, Moving Forward. Annual report of the National Chlamydia Screening Programme, 2004/5* (London: Department of Health, 2005). <http://www.dh.gov.uk>
21 Balding J, *Young People in 2002: The health related behaviour questionnaire results for 37,150 young people between the ages of 10 and 15* (Exeter: Schools Health Education Unit, 2003).

Other relevant fpa factsheets

⇨ *The law on sex.*
⇨ *Teenage pregnancy (UK).*
⇨ *Teenage pregnancy (Northern Ireland).*

Further information

For further information on the material covered in this article, and other subjects related to sexual health, contact **fpa**'s Library and Information Service. Email: library&information@**fpa**.org.uk. Tel: 020 7608 5282

⇨ The above information is reprinted with kind permission from **fpa** (formerly the Family Planning Association). For more information on this and other issues, please visit www.fpa.org.uk

© *fpa*

Information on teenage pregnancy

Information from the Department for Education and Skills

More teenage girls get pregnant in Britain than anywhere else in Europe. It's a controversial topic and experts argue about why this should be and what to do about it.

The main method used by the Government to measure teenage pregnancy is the rate of conception for all girls under 18. The rate is expressed as the number of pregnancies per 1,000 females.

Research shows that teenage mums are less likely to finish their education and get a decent job. They are also more likely to become single parents and live in poverty. Their children are at greater risk of poor health and of becoming teenage mothers themselves. Letting so many teenagers drop out of education and employment creates a major cost to our society and economy.

UK rates highest in Europe

In the 1970s, Britain had similar teenage pregnancy rates to the rest of Europe. But while other countries got theirs down in the 1980s and 1990s, Britain's rate stayed high. The latest available figures show that Britain's teenage birth rate is five times that in Holland, three times higher than in France and double the rate in Germany. Other English-

speaking countries such as Canada and New Zealand have teenage birth rates higher than ours. In the United States the rate is more than double that in the UK.

Research shows that teenage mums are less likely to finish their education and get a decent job. They are also more likely to become single parents and live in poverty

---

In 1999 the Government published a Teenage Pregnancy Report from its Social Exclusion Unit. It acknowledged there was no single cause, but pointed out three major factors: first, that many young people think they will end up on benefit anyway so they see no reason not to get pregnant. Second, that teenagers don't know enough about contraception and about what becoming a parent will involve. Third, that young people are bombarded with sexual images in the media but feel they can't talk about sex to their parents and teachers.

The Social Exclusion Unit's report set out a Teenage Pregnancy Strategy to try and tackle the problem. The aim is to cut pregnancy rates among 15-17-year-olds in England by half between 1998 and 2010. A midway goal for 2004 was also set to get rates down by 15%.

Current statistics

The latest data from the Office for National Statistics came out on 26 May 2005, published in *Health Statistics Quarterly*. They show that the pregnancy rate for under-18s in England and Wales fell to 42.3 conceptions per 1,000 girls in 2003, down from 42.8 in 2002 and about 10% lower than in 1998. But for 13-15-year-olds, the rate went up between 2002 and 2003, from 7.9 to 8.0 conceptions per thousand.

How Government is tackling the problem

The Government has set up the Teenage Pregnancy Unit to implement the Social Exclusion Unit's report. It is a cross-departmental unit located within the Department for Education and Skills. Initiatives have been launched at national and local level. The Government has made advice available to parents through helplines and its Sure Start programme. Schools have been given new guidance on sex and relationships education and better health service standards have been set for giving advice on contraceptives.

Speaking to the *Guardian* newspaper after the latest pregnancy figures, Beverley Hughes, Minister for Children, Young People and Families, acknowledged the Government can't solve the problem alone: 'We need parents to see themselves as making a unique and vital contribution to this issue. It is a contribution that I don't think anyone else can actually make.'

⇨ The above information is reprinted with kind permission from the Department for Education and Skills. Visit www.dfes.gov.uk for more information.

Teenage pregnancy

Information from fpa

This article covers government policy and key statistics on teenage pregnancy in England, Wales, Scotland and Northern Ireland (United Kingdom/UK). Please note that the data for each country may not be strictly comparable due to differences in methods of data collection and analysis.

⇨ The UK has the highest teenage birth and abortion rates in Western Europe.[1,2]

⇨ Rates of teenage births are five times those in Switzerland, four times those in the Netherlands and three times those in Finland.[2]

⇨ The US teenage pregnancy rate is nearly double the UK rate – 84 per 1,000 15-19-year-olds in 2000.[3]

⇨ Groups who are more vulnerable to becoming teenage parents include young people who are: in or leaving care, homeless, underachieving at school, children of teenage parents, members of some ethnic groups, involved in crime, living in areas with higher social deprivation.[4]

⇨ Young women living in socially disadvantaged areas are less likely to opt for an abortion if they get pregnant.[5]

putting sexual health on the agenda

England

⇨ Following a report from the Social Exclusion Unit[6] in 1998, the Teenage Pregnancy Unit was set up and a ten-year strategy and action plan was implemented.

⇨ The target is to halve the under-18 conception rate by 2010 (from 46.6 per 1,000 in 1998) and to bring about a decline in the rate of conceptions to under-16s.

⇨ The aim is also to increase the participation of teenage parents in education, employment or training to reduce their long-term risk of social exclusion.

⇨ An Independent Advisory Group on Teenage Pregnancy was established in 2002 to provide advice to the Government and monitor overall success of the strategy.[7]

⇨ Between 1998 and 2004 the teenage conception rate fell by 11.1% in under-18s and by 15.0% in under-16s.

Wales

⇨ As part of a general sexual health strategy, the Government aims to reduce teenage pregnancy rates[9] and has developed an action plan to achieve this.[10]

⇨ Between 2000 and 2004 the teenage conception rate fell by 7.8% in under-18s and by 14.8% in under-16s.

Scotland

⇨ The National Sexual Health Strategy for Scotland[13] includes the aim to reduce unintended pregnancies. There is no specific target for reducing teenage pregnancy.

The UK has the highest teenage birth and abortion rates in Western Europe

---

Northern Ireland

⇨ The Government aims to reduce the rate of births to teenage mothers by 20%, and the rate of births to teenage mothers under 17 by 40% by 2007 (compared with 2000).[15]

⇨ The strategy and action plan also aims to minimise the adverse consequences of teenage parenthood through, for example, increasing participation in education.[15]

⇨ Conception data is not available for Northern Ireland, due to the lack of complete data on the number of women having abortions. Abortion is only legal in exceptional circumstances and many women travel to England to have an abortion.

- In 2004, 225 women aged under 20 travelled to England to have an abortion,[16] compared with 301 in 2000, although these numbers are likely to be an underestimate.
- In 2004, there were 1,486 teenage births (under 20), 2.3% of 15-19-year-olds. The percentage has fallen by 11.5% since 2000.

References

1 UNICEF, *A League Table of Teenage Births in Rich Nations* (Florence: Innocenti Research Centre, 2001).

2 Bajos N et al, *Reproductive Health Behaviour of Young Europeans. Vol 1* (Strasbourg: Council of Europe, 2003).

3 Alan Guttmacher Institute, *US Teenage Pregnancy Statistics. Updates February 2004.* <http://www.guttmacher.org>

4 Swann C et al, *Teenage Pregnancy and Parenthood: A review of reviews. Evidence briefing* (London: Health Development Agency, 2003). <http://www.publichealth.nice.org.uk>

5 Lee E et al, *A Matter of Choice? Explaining national variation in teenage abortion and motherhood* (York: Joseph Rowntree Foundation, 2004). <http://www.jrf.org.uk>

6 Social Exclusion Unit. *Teenage Pregnancy.* Cm 4342 (London: Stationery Office, 1999). <http:// www.dfes.gov.uk>

7 Independent Advisory Group on Teenage Pregnancy, *Annual reports.* <http://www.dfes.gov.uk>

8 Teenage Pregnancy Unit, *Teenage Conceptions for England 1998-2004.* <http://www.dfes.gov.uk>

9 National Assembly for Wales, *A Strategic Framework for Promoting Sexual Health in Wales* (Cardiff: NAW, 2000).

Young women living in socially disadvantaged areas are less likely to opt for an abortion if they get pregnant

10 National Assembly for Wales, *A Strategic Framework for Promoting Sexual Health in Wales: Post-consultation action plan* (Cardiff: NAW, 2000). <http://www.cmo.wales.gov.uk>

11 National Assembly for Wales, *Teenage Conception Rates.* <http://www.cmo.wales.gov.uk>

12 Office for National Statistics. Unpublished data.

13 Scottish Executive, *Respect and Responsibility: Strategy and action plan for improving sexual health* (Edinburgh: Scottish Executive, 2005). <http://www.scotland.gov.uk>

14 ISD Scotland, Teenage Pregnancy. <http://www.isdscotland.org>

15 Northern Ireland, Department of Health, Social Services and Public Safety, *Teenage Pregnancy and Parenthood: Strategy and action plan 2002-2007* (Belfast: DHSSPS, 2002). <http://www.dhsspsni.gov.uk>

16 Department of Health, Abortion statistics, England and Wales: 2004 (London: DH, 2005). Statistical Bulletin 2005/11. <http://www.dh.gov.uk>

Other relevant fpa factsheets

- *Teenagers: sexual health and behaviour.*
- *Teenage pregnancy (Northern Ireland).*

Further information

For further information on the material covered in this article, and other subjects related to sexual health, contact **fpa**'s Library and Information Service. Email: library&information@fpa.org.uk. Tel: 020 7923 5228.
March 2006

- The above information is reprinted with kind permission from **fpa**. Visit www.fpa.org.uk for more information.

© *fpa*

Statistics taken from the fpa factsheet *Teenage Pregnancy*

Under-18 conceptions in England

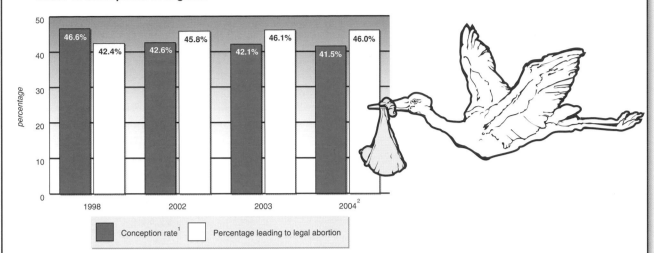

percentage

- 46.6% (1998)
- 42.4%
- 42.6% (2002)
- 45.8%
- 42.1% (2003)
- 46.1%
- 41.5% (2004²)
- 46.0%

■ Conception rate[1] □ Percentage leading to legal abortion

1. Per 1,000 females aged 15-17.
2. Provisional.

Source: Teenage Pregnancy Unit, Teenage Conceptions for England 1998-2004. *Crown copyright*

Under-16 conceptions in England

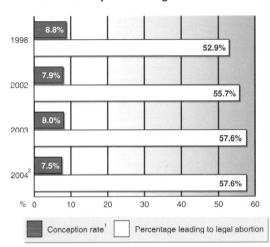

- 1998: 8.8% / 52.9%
- 2002: 7.9% / 55.7%
- 2003: 8.0% / 57.6%
- 2004²: 7.5% / 57.6%

■ Conception rate[1] □ Percentage leading to legal abortion

1. Per 1,000 females aged 13-15.
2. Provisional.

Source: Teenage Pregnancy Unit, Teenage Conceptions for England 1998-2004. *Crown copyright*

Under-16 conceptions in Wales

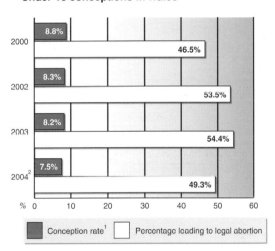

- 2000: 8.8% / 46.5%
- 2002: 8.3% / 53.5%
- 2003: 8.2% / 54.4%
- 2004²: 7.5% / 49.3%

■ Conception rate[1] □ Percentage leading to legal abortion

1. Per 1,000 females aged 13-15.
2. Provisional.

Sources: National Assembly for Wales, Teenage Conception Rates; *Office for National Statistics (unpublished data). Crown copyright*

Conceptions to 16-19-year-olds in Scotland

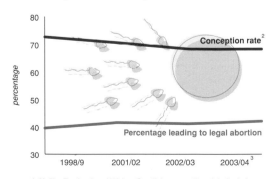

Conception rate[2]

Percentage leading to legal abortion

1. Unlike England and Wales, Scottish conception data includes miscarriages managed in hospital, as well as registered births and abortions.
2. Per 1,000 females aged 16-19.
3. Provisional.

Source: ISD Scotland, Teenage Pregnancy.

Under-16 conceptions in Scotland

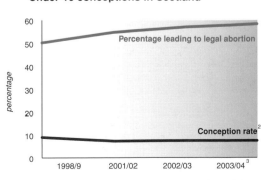

Percentage leading to legal abortion

Conception rate[2]

1. Unlike England and Wales, Scottish conception data includes miscarriages managed in hospital, as well as registered births and abortions.
2. Per 1,000 females aged 13-15.
3. Provisional.

Source: ISD Scotland, Teenage Pregnancy.

Teenage pregnancy – what to do

Information from Marie Stopes International

If your period is late and you think you might be pregnant take the following steps . . .

Do a pregnancy test

They are FREE at Brook Centres, some GPs, many family planning clinics and at some GUM clinics... the testing is confidential and only you and the nurse will know what's going on.

Hate the idea of talking to someone? For about £10 you can buy a home pregnancy test – all you do is go to your local pharmacy or supermarket where they sell a range of reliable testing kits. Follow the instructions carefully though if you want a reliable result.

The result will either be:
⇨ NEGATIVE – if you don't want to be pregnant you will breathe a sigh of relief and use this false alarm to get your contraception sorted out! See your GP, family planning clinic or use condoms.
⇨ POSITIVE – you now need to decide what to do. Other people/ doctors/counsellors can help you make a decision by explaining your choices but in the end you must decide what YOU want.

Your choices
⇨ keep the baby
⇨ adoption
⇨ abortion

Who can you talk to?

If you are pregnant, and the pregnancy is unplanned you may be feeling confused, shocked, and scared but try not to let this stop you from seeking help. It is important to face what is happening and seek advice as soon as possible, so all options are open to you and you can begin your maternity care.

It is also important to make the right decision for you, and this might not always be the decision your boyfriend or your parents would make. Try and talk it over with someone you trust.

Talking it over

You could talk it over with your boyfriend or your mum or dad, but if you don't feel you can talk to them, you could also speak to: an older sister or brother, your friends, a teacher, a doctor, a social worker, a school counsellor, your GP, Brook Advisory Counsellor, or Marie Stopes International (MSI) counsellor.

If you're old enough to do 'it' you're old enough to be responsible for what can happen

---

Whoever you talk to it's important to seek help from organisations that are impartial. For example, anti-abortion organisations will not provide unbiased or objective information.

How does pregnancy happen?

Pregnancy (conception) occurs when a sperm fertilises an egg by joining with it during sex. This can happen when two people have sex and do not use contraception.

A fertilised egg will then move down into a girl's uterus and implant itself into the womb (uterus) lining where it will begin to grow.

Are you old enough to do it?

If you're old enough to do 'it' you're old enough to be responsible for what can happen.

Whether you're male or female, with the decision to have sex, comes the responsibility of being sensible and protecting yourself from an unplanned pregnancy.

This basically means understanding how pregnancy happens and how you can stop it.

If you've got an appointment to have a pregnancy test at a clinic – don't forget...
⇨ The date of the first day of your last period.
⇨ Some of your first wee that morning – in a clean jar with a tight fitting lid.
⇨ Most clinics offer a pregnancy testing service for free – but check before you go.
⇨ If you're doing the test yourself remember to follow the instructions carefully – if you don't it could affect the results!

Keeping the baby

What happens if I decide to keep the baby?

First, see a GP who will organise maternity care for you, tell you what to expect, what you should be eating and what check-ups you need to go for.

If you are bringing up the baby on your own and need somewhere to live, you need to contact social services (your GP may be able to do this for you). Social services will be able to give you advice about benefits that you may be entitled to.

Specific organisations exist to help single parents.

Having the baby adopted

What happens if I put the baby up for adoption?

First, contact your local social services department (your GP will be able to help you).

You cannot arrange the adoption yourself unless your child is to be adopted by a close relative.

When does the adoption process begin?

Social services will work with approved adoption agencies to arrange preparation for adoption before your child is born, but nothing will be definitely arranged until after the birth. You will be completely free to change your mind.

The social worker will discuss with you the kind of family you want your child to grow up in and will usually tell you quite a lot about the family that is likely to become the baby's new parents.

You should talk to the social worker about the possibility of meeting the family, if you want to, or about other sorts of contact you could have in the future.

When does the adoption process become legal?
Although social workers arrange adoptions, they are made legally binding by the courts.

The court will make sure that you are definite about your decision to put your baby up for adoption and that the baby's new home is the right environment for him/her to grow up in.

The adoption is usually made legal three months after the birth of the child.

What if I change my mind?
Everyone recognises that putting a child up for adoption is a very big step for a mother so you have at least six weeks after the birth before you need to give your final agreement in writing to the court.

When the adoption order has been agreed by the court you will no longer have any legal relationship with or responsibilities for your child.

Is adoption the same as fostering?
No, adoption means legally giving up responsibility for your child. Fostering means that another set of parents will temporarily look after your baby but that you will remain the legal guardian and hopefully be in a position to care for your child in the future.

The same people who organise adoption can help you with fostering. If, for whatever reason, you cannot look after your baby, social services will arrange temporary fostering and will try to work with you to reunite you with your child. Making a decision about adoption or fostering is a big one and you should feel able to take time to make the right decision for you and speak to organisations

and people who can help you make up your mind.

For more help and advice on adoption contact:
The British Agencies for Adoption and Fostering (BAAF)
11 Southwark Street, London SE1 1RQ
Tel: 0207 593 2000

Abortion: ending the pregnancy

What happens if I decide to have an abortion?
Firstly, see your GP, MSI or Brook for information about the type of abortion available to you.

You could also ask to see a counsellor at the clinic as they will go through the feelings you may have before and after.

If you are pregnant, and the pregnancy is unplanned you may be feeling confused, shocked, and scared but try not to let this stop you from seeking help

---

Their aim is to help you cope with what you are going through and help you make the right decision. Both the doctor and the counsellor will discuss if you want your parents to know about your abortion.

While you can give consent (agree to an abortion) under 16, a doctor will only give the go-ahead if s/he believes you understand what's involved.

Even if a doctor agrees, they may still encourage you to involve a parent (though they will not go behind your back and tell your parents).

Who can I take with me?
Lots of women prefer to go with someone to support them. You can take anyone, from a friend, a relative, or a parent to a boyfriend or a brother or sister.

Abortion options: what kind of abortion are there?
What kind of abortion you have very much depends on:
⇨ how many weeks pregnant you are

⇨ whether or not you want a general anaesthetic (without one you will be awake during the procedure)
⇨ whether or not you are suitable for a medical abortion (you will be given pills to end your pregnancy).

The earlier you go for help the more options are available so don't put off seeking advice.

Remember, you have choices so make sure that all options are clearly explained to you by the nurse/doctor and don't be afraid to ask questions.

What happens afterwards?
After you have ended your pregnancy you will probably feel cramps very like your period cramps, and experience some bleeding which can last up to 14 days.

The nurses will tell you what to expect, and how to look after yourself. They will also make you a follow-up appointment to make sure there are no problems.

Finally, a doctor will also discuss having sex again. While this may be the last thing on your mind, you need to know how long to wait after your abortion and what contraception to use. If you want to talk to someone after your abortion most hospitals and organisations like MSI offer post-abortion counselling.

⇨ The above information is reprinted with kind permission from Marie Stopes International. Visit www.likeitis.org for more information.
© Marie Stopes International

Consequences of teenage births

Long-term consequences of teenage births for parents and their children

What are the longer-term effects of having a child as a teenager? New research from the Institute of Social and Economic Research, University of Essex, has used recent birth cohort and household panel datasets to explore the 'causal effects' of teenage motherhood, looking at a wide range of possible consequences for both mother and child. Their findings take account of associations arising partly from the fact that already-disadvantaged teenagers have a higher risk of having a baby.

Key findings

⇨ Women from poorer backgrounds and from areas with higher unemployment rates are more likely to become mothers as a teenager – e.g. women whose fathers were in manual occupations were nearly twice as likely to have a child as a

---

Women whose fathers were in manual occupations were nearly twice as likely to have a child as a teenager than those whose fathers were in non-manual occupations

---

teenager than those whose fathers were in non-manual occupations, and a percentage point higher unemployment rate increases the percentage of women becoming teenage mothers from 13% to 14%.

⇨ A new and more rigorous analytical approach shows that the negative consequences of having a teen-birth for the mother are not as wide-ranging as earlier research suggested.

⇨ The primary consequence for mothers is that women having a teen-birth fare worse in the 'marriage market' in the sense that they partner with men who are poorly qualified and more likely to suffer unemployment. Compared to postponing childbearing beyond her teens, the probability that a teen-mother's partner does not have education beyond 16 rises from about 60% to 80% and the probability that he has a job falls from 95% to 75%. This reduces their standard of living.

⇨ Teenage mothers suffer from poorer mental health in the three years after their birth compared with other mothers – they have 30% higher levels of mental illness 2 years after the birth, after which they start to converge to the population average.

⇨ The association of early childbearing with economic disadvantage is smaller, or non-existent, for ethnic minority groups who are already substantially disadvantaged.

⇨ Children of teenage mothers suffer as young adults in terms of lower educational attainment, a higher risk of economic inactivity and of becoming a teenage mother themselves. This may result because of the lower standard of living experienced by many teenage mothers, owing in part to the poorer earning partners that they pair with.

⇨ The above information is an extract from the research briefing *Long-term Consequences of Teenage Births for Parents and Their Children* published by the Teenage Pregnancy Unit and is reprinted with permission. Visit www.dfes.gov.uk/teenagepregnancy to view the full document.

- WE'RE LIKE SISTERS!!

... EXCEPT ONE OF US HAS STILL GOT TO BE THE PARENT...

Statistics: teen pregnancy and lone parenthood

Percentage of births outside marriage: EU comparison

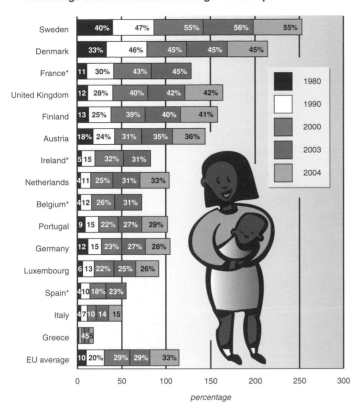

Country	1980	1990	2000	2003	2004
Sweden	40%	47%	55%	56%	55%
Denmark	33%	46%	45%	45%	45%
France*	11	30%	43%	45%	
United Kingdom	12	28%	40%	42%	42%
Finland	13	25%	39%	40%	41%
Austria	18%	24%	31%	35%	36%
Ireland*	5	15	32%	31%	
Netherlands	4	11	25%	31%	33%
Belgium*	4	12	26%	31%	
Portugal	9	15	22%	27%	29%
Germany	12	15	23%	27%	28%
Luxembourg	6	13	22%	25%	26%
Spain*	4	10	18%	23%	
Italy	4	7	10	14	15
Greece	1	4	5	5	
EU average	10	20%	29%	29%	33%

*2004 data unavailable.

Source: ONS (2006); Social Trends 36. Crown copyright. Sourced from OnePlusOne.

Most teenage mothers worldwide (aged 15-19)

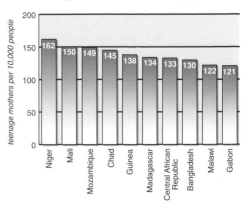

teenage mothers per 10,000 people

Niger 162, Mali 150, Mozambique 149, Chad 145, Guinea 138, Madagascar 134, Central African Republic 133, Bangladesh 130, Malawi 122, Gabon 121

Fewest teenage mothers worldwide (aged 15-19)

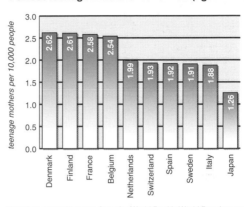

teenage mothers per 10,000 people

Denmark 2.62, Finland 2.61, France 2.58, Belgium 2.54, Netherlands 1.99, Switzerland 1.93, Spain 1.92, Sweden 1.91, Italy 1.88, Japan 1.26

Technical notes: Data are from the World Bank's World Development Indicators 2005, and the United Nations Fund for Children – Innocenti Research Centre Report Card. Rates less than 1 in 10000 were not ranked; this includes China, Taiwan, the Republic of Korea, Hong Kong, Mongolia, and DPR Korea. Sourced from www.worldmapper.org

Number of teenage conceptions: by age of conception and outcome, England and Wales, 2001.

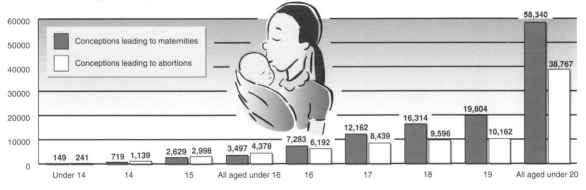

Conceptions leading to maternities / Conceptions leading to abortions

Age	Maternities	Abortions
Under 14	149	241
14	719	1,139
15	2,629	2,998
All aged under 16	3,497	4,378
16	7,283	6,192
17	12,162	8,439
18	16,314	9,596
19	19,804	10,162
All aged under 20	58,340	38,767

Source: ONS (2005); Social Trends 35. Crown copyright. Sourced from OnePlusOne.

Financial situation for two adults working 35 hours per week at minimum wage and one 12-year-old child in various household situations

	Both parents & child living together	First parent & child living together	Second parent living separately
Earnings	£16,424	£8,212	£8,212
Disposable income after tax and benefits	£16,791	£12,567	£8,240
Government subsidy[1]	£367	£4,355	£28
Equivalence scale value[2]	1.26	0.86	0.61
Standard of living before housing costs[3]	£13,432	£14,612	£13,508
Standard of living after housing costs[4]	£10,693	£11,689	£9,818

1. Does not include amount of income tax and national insurance cancelled by tax credits (£1,900.76 for both parents and child living together and £950.38 in the other two cases).
2. Before housing costs.
3. Based on McClements Equivalisation Scale as used in Department for Work and Pensions, Households Below Average Income, 1994/95-2001/02, CDS, Leeds, 2003.
4. Housing costs based on Dept. for Work and Pensions, Tax Benefit Model Tables, April 2003. Assumes each example is living in local authority housing.

Source: Civitas; from the press release 'Tax credits favour lone parenthood', 2006.

Sex education and teenage pregnancy

Information from the Department for Education and Skills

Girls who give birth as teenagers are more likely to experience poverty, and young people are also particularly vulnerable to some sexually transmitted infections such as chlamydia – two reasons why Sex and Relationship Education (SRE) in schools is a key part of pupils' Personal, Social and Health Education.

SRE aims to build an understanding of human sexuality, and to provide young people with the confidence, knowledge and skills to make informed and responsible choices.

Schools produce their own SRE programmes, taking into account Government guidance and the views of parents. The guidance makes clear that SRE in schools should:

⇨ recognise the importance of marriage and stable relationships;

⇨ be age-appropriate;

⇨ help to reduce the rate of teenage pregnancy.

At the appropriate age, the issues covered should include:

⇨ how to recognise and avoid abuse and exploitation;

⇨ skills to avoid being pressured into unwanted or unprotected sex;

⇨ the benefits of delaying sexual activity and avoiding risky behaviour;

⇨ safer sex.

The hope is that SRE can help to reduce the rate of sexually transmitted infections (STIs).

How are parents involved in school SRE?

The Learning and Skills Act 2000 obliges schools to consult parents when developing an SRE programme. The school's SRE policy should be available for parents to inspect. Parents can withdraw their child from SRE lessons, except where the lessons form part of the national curriculum for science.

How much of a problem is teenage pregnancy?

Teenage Pregnancy: Accelerating the Strategy to 2010, published in September 2006, reported on the progress of the Government's National Teenage Pregnancy Strategy. Based on 2004 data, rates of teenage pregnancy were at their lowest for 20 years.

Sex education in schools can be effective in reducing risky sexual behaviour

However when compared with many other developed countries, the UK's teenage pregnancy rate remains high. According to UNICEF, in 1998 the UK had the highest teenage conception rate in Europe among women under 20, with 30.8 births per 1,000 15- to 19-year-olds.

Unicef also found evidence of a strong link with social disadvantage. Based on the 13 European countries examined in the study, women who gave birth as teenagers were twice as likely to end up in poverty.

Figures from the Office of National Statistics suggest that the rate of conception for females in England aged 15-17 is falling. They show a rate of 41.5 conceptions per 1,000 females aged 15-17 in 2004, a reduction of 11.1 percentage points from 1998.

How much of a problem are STIs among young people?

The 2005 Health Protection Agency figures on STIs indicate that infection rates continue to rise in the UK population overall:

⇨ new diagnoses at genito-urinary medicine clinics were up 3% from 2004;

⇨ young people are disproportionately affected by some infections;

⇨ the rates of chlamydia infection were highest for the 16-24 age group.

Can SRE improve young people's sexual health and help prevent teenage pregnancies?

Academics from the Institute of Education and Keele University reported that schools, along with parents, are young people's main source of information about sex. Another review carried out for the Health Development Agency concluded that sex education in schools can be effective in reducing risky sexual behaviour.

What type of SRE is most effective?

According to the 2004 Social Exclusion Unit report, opinions differ over what form of SRE is most effective. The previous year, the Health Development Agency found some evidence that individual programmes focusing on personal development, self-esteem

and negotiation skills may increase contraceptive use.

Schools, along with parents, are young people's main source of information about sex

---

By contrast, the *British Medical Journal* published results of a study in 2002 which suggested that this sort of programme has some limitations. It compared children who had taken the course with those who had received conventional sex education and found:

⇨ an apparent increased knowledge of sexual health;

⇨ no difference in sexual activity.

The study's authors suggested that possible reasons for this might include the relatively short time-frame (20 lessons over two school years). Another possibility was that the programme was relatively

unimportant compared with other influences, such as family.

The Health Development Agency report concluded that two features of effective programmes are:

⇨ a long-term approach;

⇨ parental involvement.

Where can I find out more?

The Department for Education and Skills provides further information on SRE for parents and carers as does ParentsCentre.

The Government's need2know website offers information on sex and relationships for young people.

More research and resources as well as information on the National Teenage Pregnancy Strategy can be found on the website of the Government's Teenage Pregnancy Unit.

⇨ The above information is re-printed with kind permission from the Department for Education and Skills. Visit www.dfes.gov.uk for more information.

© Crown copyright

Sex education that works

Information from AVERT

What is sex education?

Sex education, which is sometimes called sexuality education or sex and relationships education, is the process of acquiring information and forming attitudes and beliefs about sex, sexual identity, relationships and intimacy. It is also about developing young people's skills so that they make informed choices about their behaviour, and feel confident and competent about

acting on these choices. It is widely accepted that young people have a right to sex education, partly because it is a means by which they are helped to protect themselves against abuse, exploitation, unintended pregnancies, sexually transmitted diseases and HIV/AIDS.

What are the aims of sex education?

Sex education seeks both to reduce the risks of potentially negative outcomes from sexual behaviour like unwanted or unplanned pregnancies and infection with sexually transmitted diseases, and to enhance the quality of relationships. It is also about developing young people's ability to make decisions over their

entire lifetime. Sex education that works, by which we mean that it is effective, is sex education that contributes to this overall aim.

What skills should sex education develop?

If sex education is going to be effective it needs to include opportunities for young people to develop skills, as it can be hard for them to act on the basis of only having information. The kinds of skills young people develop as part of sex education are linked to more general life-skills. For example, being able to communicate, listen, negotiate, ask for and identify sources of help and advice, are useful life-skills and can be applied in terms of sexual relationships. Effective sex education develops young people's skills in negotiation, decision-making, assertion and listening. Other important skills include being

Sex education that works starts early

able to recognise pressures from other people and to resist them, deal with and challenge prejudice, seek help from adults – including parents, carers and professionals – through the family, community and health and welfare services. Sex education that works also helps equip young people with the skills to be able to differentiate between accurate and inaccurate information, discuss a range of moral and social issues and perspectives on sex and sexuality, including different cultural attitudes and sensitive issues like sexuality, abortion and contraception.

Forming attitudes and beliefs

Young people can be exposed to a wide range of attitudes and beliefs in relation to sex and sexuality. These sometimes appear contradictory and confusing. For example, some health messages emphasise the risks and dangers associated with sexual activity and some media coverage promotes the idea that being sexually active makes a person more attractive and mature. Because sex and sexuality are sensitive subjects, young people and sex educators can have strong views on what attitudes people should hold, and what moral framework should govern people's behaviour – these too can sometimes seem to be at odds. Young people are very interested in the moral and cultural frameworks that binds sex and sexuality. They often welcome opportunities to talk about issues where people have strong views, like abortion, sex before marriage, lesbian and gay issues and contraception and birth control. It is important to remember that talking in a balanced way about differences in opinion does not promote one set of views over another, or mean that one agrees with a particular view. Part of exploring and understanding cultural, religious and moral views is finding out that you can agree to disagree.

People providing sex education have attitudes and beliefs of their own about sex and sexuality and it is important not to let these influence negatively the sex education that they provide. For example, even if a person believes that young people should not have sex until they are married, this does not imply withholding important information about safer sex and contraception. Attempts to impose narrow moralistic views about sex and sexuality on young people through sex education have failed. Rather than trying to deter or frighten young people away from having sex, effective sex education includes work on attitudes and beliefs, coupled with skills development, that enables young people to choose whether or not to have a sexual relationship taking into account the potential risks of any sexual activity.

Effective sex education also provides young people with an opportunity to explore the reasons why people have sex, and to think about how it involves emotions, respect for oneself and other people and their feelings, decisions and bodies. Young people should have the chance to explore gender differences and how ethnicity and sexuality can influence people's feelings and options. They should be able to decide for themselves what the positive qualities of relationships are. It is important that they understand how bullying, stereotyping, abuse and exploitation can negatively influence relationships.

So what information should be given to young people?

Young people get information about sex and sexuality from a wide range of sources including each other, through the media including advertising, television and magazines, as well as leaflets, books and websites (such as www.avert.org) which are intended to be sources of information about sex and sexuality. Some of this will be accurate and some inaccurate. Providing information through sex education is therefore about finding out what young people already know and adding to their existing knowledge and correcting any misinformation they may have. For example, young people may have heard that condoms are not effective against HIV/AIDS or that there is a cure for AIDS. It is important to provide information which corrects mistaken beliefs. Without correct information young people can put themselves at greater risk.

Information is also important as the basis on which young people can develop well-informed attitudes and views about sex and sexuality. Young people need to have information on all the following topics:
⇨ Sexual development
⇨ Reproduction
⇨ Contraception
⇨ Relationships.

They need to have information about the physical and emotional changes associated with puberty and sexual reproduction, including fertilisation and conception and about sexually transmitted diseases, including HIV/AIDS. They also need to know about contraception and birth control including what contraceptives there are, how they work, how people use them, how they decide what to use or not, and how they can be obtained. In terms of information about relationships they need to know about what kinds of relationships there are, about love and commitment, marriage and partnership and the law relating to sexual behaviour and relationships as well as the range of religious and cultural views on sex and sexuality and sexual diversity. In addition, young people should be provided with information about abortion, sexuality, and confidentiality, as well as about the range of sources of advice and support that is available in the community and nationally.

When should sex education start?

Sex education that works starts early, before young people reach puberty, and before they have developed established patterns of behaviour. The precise age at which information should be provided depends on the physical, emotional and intellectual development of the young people as well as their level of understanding. What is covered and also how, depends on who is providing the sex education, when they are providing it, and in what context, as well as what the individual young person wants to know about.

It is important not to delay providing information to young people but to begin when they are young. Providing basic information provides the foundation on which more complex knowledge is built up over time. This also means that sex education has to be sustained. For example, when they are very young, children can be informed about how people grow and change over time, and how babies become children and then adults, and this provides the basis on which they understand more detailed information about puberty provided in the pre-teenage years. They can also, when they are young, be provided with information about viruses and germs that attack the body. This provides the basis for talking to them later about infections that can be caught through sexual contact.

Providing basic information provides the foundation on which more complex knowledge is built up over time.

Some people are concerned that providing information about sex and sexuality arouses curiosity and can lead to sexual experimentation. There is no evidence that this happens. It is important to remember that young people can store up information provided at any time, for a time when they need it later on.

Sometimes it can be difficult for adults to know when to raise issues, but the important thing is to maintain an open relationship with children which provides them with opportunities to ask questions when they have them. Parents and carers can also be proactive and engage young people in discussions about sex, sexuality and relationships. Naturally, many parents and their children feel embarrassed about talking about some aspects of sex and sexuality. Viewing sex education as an ongoing conversation about values, attitudes and issues as well as providing facts can be helpful. The best basis to proceed on is a sound relationship in which a young person feels able to ask a question or raise an issue if they feel they need to. It has been shown that in countries like the Netherlands, where many families regard it as an important responsibility to talk openly with children about sex and sexuality, this contributes to greater cultural openness about sex and sexuality and improved sexual health among young people.

The role of many parents and carers as sex educators changes as young people get older and young people are provided with more opportunities to receive formal sex education through schools and community settings. However, it doesn't get any less important. Because sex education in school tends to take place in blocks of time, it can't always address issues relevant to young people at a

particular time, and parents can fulfil a particularly important role in providing information and opportunities to discuss things as they arise.

Who should provide sex education?

Different settings provide different contexts and opportunities for sex education. At home, young people can easily have one-to-one discussions with parents or carers which focus on specific issues, questions or concerns. They can have a dialogue about their attitudes and views. Sex education at home also tends to take place over a long time, and involve lots of short interactions between parents and children. There may be times when young people seem reluctant to talk, but it is important not to interpret any diffidence as meaning that there is nothing left to talk about. As young people get older advantage can be taken of opportunities provided by things seen on television for example, as an opportunity to initiate conversation. It is also important not to defer dealing with a question or issue for too long as it can suggest that you are unwilling to talk about it.

In school the interaction between the teacher and young people takes a different form and is often provided in organised blocks of lessons. It is not as well suited to advising the individual as it is to providing information from an impartial point of view. The most effective sex education acknowledges the different contributions each setting can make. Schools programmes which involve parents, notifying them what is being taught and when, can support the initiation of dialogue at home. Parents and schools both need to engage with young people about the messages that they get from the media, and give them opportunities for discussion.

In some countries, the involvement of young people themselves in developing and providing sex education has increased as a means of ensuring the relevance and accessibility of provision. Consultation with young people at the point when programmes are designed, helps ensure that they are relevant and the involvement of young people in delivering programmes may reinforce messages as they model attitudes and behaviour to their peers.

Effective school-based sex education

School-based sex education can be an important and effective way of enhancing young people's knowledge, attitudes and behaviour. There is widespread agreement that formal education should include sex education and what works has been well-researched. Evidence suggests that effective school programmes will include the following elements:

⇨ A focus on reducing specific risky behaviours;

⇨ A basis in theories which explain what influences people's sexual choices and behaviour;

⇨ A clear, and continuously re-inforced message about sexual behaviour and risk reduction;

⇨ Providing accurate information about the risks associated with sexual activity, about contraception and birth control, and about methods of avoiding or deferring intercourse;

⇨ Dealing with peer and other social pressures on young people; Providing opportunities to practise communication, negotiation and assertion skills;

⇨ Uses a variety of approaches to teaching and learning that involve and engage young people and help them to personalise the information;

⇨ Uses approaches to teaching and learning which are appropriate to young people's age, experience and cultural background;

⇨ Is provided by people who believe in what they are saying and have access to support in the form of training or consultation with other sex educators.

Formal programmes with these elements have been shown to increase young people's levels of knowledge about sex and sexuality, put back the average age at which they first have sexual intercourse and decrease risk when they do have sex . All the elements are important and inter-related, and sex education needs to be supported by links to sexual health services, otherwise it is not going to be so effective. It also takes into account the messages about sexual values and behaviour young people get from other sources, like friends and the media. It is also responsive to the needs of the young people themselves – whether they are girls or boys, on their own or in a single-sex or mixed sex-group, and what they know already, their age and experiences.

⇨ The above information is an extract from information published by AVERT, the UK HIV and AIDS charity, and is reprinted with permission. Please visit the AVERT website at www.avert.org for more information on this and other issues, or to view the full article.

© AVERT

Beyond biology

Sex and relationships education must go beyond biology, says sex education forum

83 per cent of parents of school-age children think that schools should teach young people about the emotional aspects of sex and relationships as well as the biological facts, according to a new survey commissioned by the Sex Education Forum, the national authority on sex and relationships education.

The survey, carried out for the Forum by GfK NOP earlier this year, also found that 77 per cent of parents think schools should be required to provide comprehensive sex and relationships education as part of the national curriculum.

The findings support a call from the Sex Education Forum for personal, social and health education (PSHE) – which includes sex and relationships – to be compulsory. Although under current legislation schools have to teach the biological aspects of sex, there is no statutory requirement to provide PSHE, which typically includes learning about relationships and the emotional aspects of sex, as well as life skills such as decision making, managing peer pressure and understanding risky behaviour.

'There is a clear groundswell of support for making PSHE compulsory within schools,' said Anna Martinez, coordinator of the Sex Education Forum. 'Both young people and their parents have repeatedly told us that they want better school-based sex and relationships education, which meets their needs now and in the future.

'Under the current system the provision of PSHE is patchy, and in many schools it may be delivered by under-trained, poorly prepared teachers. This can have a serious impact on the decisions children and young people make in their lives, from becoming sexually active before they are ready to failing to understand the risk of unintended pregnancy or sexually transmitted infections.

'We believe that if we are to support the next generation to become competent, healthy young adults, sex and relationships education within PSHE needs to be statutory, not an optional extra.'

The Sex Education Forum plans a year-long programme to promote its call for statutory PSHE. Activities include a dedicated minisite, Beyond Biology, which includes facts and figures on sex and relationships education, and the Forum is encouraging individuals and organisations to sign up to its call for action via the site.
23 May 2006

⇨ The above information is reprinted with kind permission from NCB's Sex Education Forum. For more information on this and other issues, please visit their website at www.ncb.org.uk/sef

© NCB

Call for sex education in primary schools

Sex education in primary schools needed to cut teenage pregnancy and unprotected underage sex

Children should be taught about the importance of contraception in their last year of primary school, according to new research from the Institute for Public Policy Research (ippr) to be published next month. The report shows that British teenagers are the most sexually active in Europe and are third least likely to use a condom during underage sex.

Britain has the highest rate of births to teenagers in Europe, with an average of 26 live births per 1,000 women aged 15 to 19 – nearly a fifth higher than Latvia, the country with the next highest rate, and more than four times the rate of Cyprus, Slovenia, Sweden and Denmark. Despite concerted efforts from Government and a target to halve teenage pregnancy rates between 1999 and 2010, progress remains frustratingly slow: there were 41.4 conceptions per thousand women under the age of 18 in 2005 – just 2.9 per thousand lower than in 1991.

The report shows that almost one in three 15-year-olds didn't use a condom during their last sexual intercourse. It shows that British teenagers' sexual health is considerably poorer than it was a decade ago. In the last ten years:

⇨ Levels of genital chlamydia rose by 508 for male and 238 per cent for female teenagers.

⇨ Levels of genital herpes rose by 52 for male and 38 per cent for female teenagers.

⇨ Levels of syphilis increased nearly 16 fold for males and 14 fold for female teenagers.

ippr's report, *Freedom's Orphans: Raising Youth in a Changing World*, will be published next month (Nov) and will recommend:

⇨ Teenagers should be offered a full choice of contraception,

including long-lasting forms – like the Norplant implant which last three years. Condoms should be widely available at low cost, or no cost, to young people in places that they use and are accessible to them: sports facilities, schools and further education colleges.

⇨ Personal, Social and Health Education (PSHE) including sex and relationship education should become a statutory subject in all primary and secondary schools in England and Wales.

⇨ Services for parents, including information on parenting and childcare, access to parenting groups and more specialised support for parents who want and would benefit from it, should be offered at every school, when it extends its opening hours from 8am-6pm.

⇨ Access to support and information for teenage mothers and teenagers who have had abortions should be improved, in order to tackle the number of teenagers experiencing second pregnancies.

Julia Margo, ippr Senior Research Fellow, said:

'Over the last 50 years, the average age of first sexual intercourse has fallen from 20 for men and 21 for women in the 1950s to 16 by the mid-1990s. The proportion of young people who are sexually active before the age of consent has risen from less than one per cent to 25 per cent over the same period. Our education system must respond in kind and start teaching children about the risks involved in sex before they even consider taking those risks.'

23 October 2006

⇨ The above information is reprinted with kind permission from the Institute for Public Policy Research. Visit www.ippr.org.uk for more information.

© *ippr*

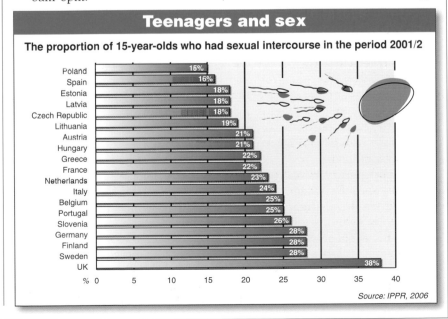

Teenagers and sex

The proportion of 15-year-olds who had sexual intercourse in the period 2001/2

Country	%
Poland	15%
Spain	16%
Estonia	18%
Latvia	18%
Czech Republic	18%
Lithuania	19%
Austria	21%
Hungary	21%
Greece	22%
France	22%
Netherlands	23%
Italy	24%
Belgium	25%
Portugal	25%
Slovenia	26%
Germany	28%
Finland	28%
Sweden	28%
UK	38%

Source: IPPR, 2006

Mum's the word

Survey reveals difference in attitudes towards young mums

As Mothers' Day approaches, a survey by a leading young women's charity reveals that while we might think we are a nation which respects mothers, when it comes to teenage mums we are still as prejudiced as ever.

A new NOP survey, commissioned by YWCA England & Wales, found that while we overwhelmingly agree that love rather than age is the key to being a good mum, most of us don't think that teenage mums are up to the job.

The poll compared public reaction to the word mum versus the phrase teenage mum. The results found that while 95 per cent of people think that love and compassion are more important than age when it comes to being a good mother, teenage mums were almost six times more likely to be described as incapable.

Moreover, while over 90 per cent of people associated the word mum with being loving, devoted, responsible and capable, put the word teenage in front of it and there is an entirely different response:

⇨ only 49 per cent of respondents think teenage mums are responsible (compared to 91 per cent for mums in general)

⇨ just 64 per cent think they are devoted (compared to 91 per cent for mums in general)

⇨ seven times as many respondents described teenage mums as irresponsible

⇨ three times as many people labelled teenage mums 'promiscuous'.

Conducted as part of YWCA's RESPECT young mums campaign, the survey aims to challenge the assumptions many of us wrongly make about young mums.

'There's no evidence to suggest that younger mums are any less capable than older mums. In fact, our experience shows that they are just as able to be good parents. Despite this, they still face prejudice and discrimination,' says Sophie Holmes, director of policy, research and campaigns at YWCA England & Wales. 'Research has shown that the majority want to get work and create a secure future for themselves and their children, but this is rarely acknowledged. It's time we gave young mums they respect they deserve.'

Tamara Shaul, a young mum, says 'I wouldn't change a thing about being a young mum – it's wonderful and so rewarding. But I'd like to change people's attitudes. People assume that the older you are the better you'll be but parenting isn't about your age, it's about your ability to do it. You're either a good mum or you're not.'

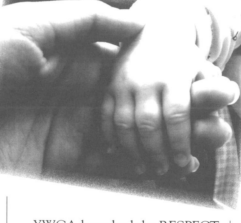

YWCA launched the RESPECT young mums campaign in September 2004. It challenges the poverty and prejudice faced by young mums and calls for young mums to have the same rights, access to healthcare and education as other mums, and to ensure that they are treated equally and with respect. On Mother's Day, the charity is urging people to sign up to its young mums' charter to show support for teenage mums.

A previous poll revealed that 49 per cent of the public think that young women get pregnant to get a council house or for benefits. In fact 70 per cent of 15- to 16-year-olds who are pregnant or have a baby still live with their parents or carers, as do around 50 per cent of 17- to 18-year-olds.

Other research shows that:

⇨ the majority of teenage mums live in poverty and nearly half of teenage parents are in the bottom fifth of the income distribution

⇨ half of education professionals think that young mums are not interested in education, when the reality is that pregnancy increases young women's interest

⇨ 79 per cent of young mums felt motherhood increased their determination to get a good job.

The Mum's the Word poll showed that 89 per cent of people – and 92 per cent of men – agree that Mothers' Day is a day to make mum feel special. But while men might agree it's a special day for mums, it is women who are more likely to push the boat out and do something for them – including 90 per cent who said they'd send a card or flowers and 45 per cent who said they'd even do her housework.

Other findings from the Mum's the Word poll:

⇨ the younger generation (25-44) is more likely to recognise capability in teenage mums than their older counterparts

⇨ the older generation (55-65+) is more likely to view teenage mums as irresponsible and promiscuous

⇨ 86 per cent of us will send our mum a card or flowers on Mother's Day, 52 per cent will treat her to a meal out, 23 per cent will give her breakfast in bed and 2 per cent will do nothing at all

⇨ young people are more likely to help their mums out on Mother's Day, 58 per cent of 15- to 24-year-olds said they would do the housework and 41 per cent said they would take her breakfast in bed.

28 February 2005

⇨ The above information is reprinted with kind permission from the YWCA. Visit www.ywca-gb.org.uk for more information.

© YWCA

Pregnancy in teenage girls 'all part of nature's law'

⇨ *Leading doctor points out role of evolutionary programming in pregnancies*

⇨ *Remarks branded 'flippant' and 'outrageous' by politicians and church group*

⇨ *Abortions among under-16s have reached record levels in Scotland*

'Society may "tut tut" about them, but their actions are part of an evolutionary process that goes back nearly two million years; while their behaviour may not fit with western society's expectations, it is perhaps useful to consider it in a wider context.' – Dr Lawrence Shaw

A leading doctor sparked controversy last night after claiming teenage girls who get pregnant 'behind the bike sheds' are only obeying nature's law and should not be condemned out of hand.

Dr Laurence Shaw, deputy medical director of the Bridge Centre fertility clinic in London, said females had been programmed by two million years of evolution to have babies in their late teens and early twenties, when fertility is at its peak.

Speaking at the annual meeting of the European Society of Human Reproduction and Embryology (Eshre), he said nature intended women to become mothers when young, and for their fertility to decline while they raised their children.

But last night family groups and politicians in Scotland, which has western Europe's highest rate of teenage pregnancy, condemned his view.

Figures published last month revealed that abortions among under-16s have reached record levels, with 341 terminations in Scotland last year.

Speaking to delegates in Prague, Dr Shaw said: 'Before we condemn our teenagers for having sex behind the bike sheds and becoming pregnant, we should remember that this is a

By Jonathan Lessware

natural response by these girls to their rising fertility levels.

'Society may "tut tut" about them, but their actions are part of an evolutionary process that goes back nearly two million years; while their behaviour may not fit with western society's expectations, it is perhaps useful to consider it in a wider context.'

> **'Society may "tut tut" about [pregnant teenagers], but their actions are part of an evolutionary process that goes back nearly two million years'**

Shona Robison, the SNP's health spokeswoman, whose constituency in Dundee has rates of teenage pregnancy far exceeding the national average, called the remarks 'flippant'.

'Maybe he should reflect on the effects of teenage pregnancy,' she said. 'In representing Dundee, I am well aware of the problems teenage pregnancy can cause girls. For many it leads to a life of poverty and a loss of opportunity. I doubt these are the things he would want for his own daughters.'

Teresa Smith, chair of the Scottish Christian People's Alliance, said the comments were 'completely outrageous'.

'Many things are an occurrence within nature but it does not mean they are the right thing to do,' she said. 'Girls of that age are not mature enough to bring up a baby. If they choose to have an abortion, there are long-term effects.

'Teenagers having sexual activity risk catching chlamydia and causing fertility problems. We should be promoting abstinence, not telling young people this is natural.'

Tim Street, the chief executive, of the Family Planning Association Scotland, said the comments highlighted the need to educate teenagers about the dangers of sex.

'We have to actually explain to young people that we want them to wait until they are older before they start having sex and eventually kids.

'If, as he says, this is a natural, biological reaction to being who you are, we also have to explain that good policies on this are about delaying sexual intercourse until later on.'

In his talk Dr Shaw also said it was wrong to be prejudiced against older women who sought fertility treatment.

'Before we criticise 62-year-old women who want to have babies, we should remember that it was not so long ago that women would only have had about 20 or 30 years to care for their offspring and help with the next generation,' he said.

19 June 2006

© *Scotsman Publications Ltd*

Poverty and yo[ung]
parenthood

**Poverty and disadvantage can push teenage[rs into]
parenthood according to new resear[ch]**

Some teenagers feel that their conscious decision to become a parent is a reasonably rational life choice given their past and the options available to them. This is according to new Joseph Rowntree Foundation research undertaken [...]

of a 'father figure' and wanting to be there for their child. They could have

[...]eir
[...]d by
[...]ildren.
[...]verybody
[...]and I knew
[...]g when I got
[...]ne 18-year-old

[...]as
[...]life,
[...]ate a
[...]eir own

[...]ood as pro-
[...]reate a loving
[...]nsating for their
[...]ces of childhood),
[...], sense of capability
[...]ion. Many said that
[...]uld have been worse if
[...]ot become a parent – due
[...]nued family disruption and
[...]ppiness, a growing sense of
[...]thlessness and lack of direction. Young fathers gave similar reasons for 'planning' but there were also differences, such as their own lack

Stopping the use of contraception was often seen as placing the prospect of pregnancy in the 'lap of the gods'. Although the interviewees understood the purpose of contraception, many were not aware that teenagers have high fertility rates. In some cases, a miscarriage had led to a 'planned' pregnancy out of fear that this could impact on their ability to have children in the future. In the report, authors suggest a need for improved support after miscarriage. They found that those 'planning' pregnancy have different support needs to those who became pregnant unintentionally.

Lead author Suzanne Cater said: 'This research has implications

[...] pregnancy reduction, [...] to identify those more [...] choose young parenthood. [...]ghting the fact that not all [...]age pregnancies are unplanned [...]l help address support needs [...]urrently not being met. Using teenagers who wish they had delayed parenthood could also help inform young people who may have potentially unrealistic expectations of parenthood.'

Dr Lester Coleman, who managed the research project, said: 'For the first time, the views and experiences of young people who "planned" their pregnancies are being heard. Their accounts will be of great value to those working to reduce teenage pregnancy and those who support young parents.'

A minority of the sample openly regretted the decision to become pregnant. Worse finances and housing, isolation and the sheer hard work were overwhelming for some. Sharing these experiences may help other young people make better-informed decisions.

In-depth interviews with 51 white young people aged 13-22 were completed in areas of high poverty and disadvantage in six different areas across England.

This article refers to information from the report 'Planned' teenage pregnancy: Perspectives of young parents from disadvantaged backgrounds *by Suzanne Cater and Lester Coleman. It is published for the Joseph Rowntree Foundation by The Policy Press.*
17 July 2006

Teenage mums should not be stigmatised

Information from the YWCA

There is no doubt that some teenage mums can benefit from support in preparing them for the practical and emotional demands of parenthood. Courses run by YWCA are enthusiastically received by pregnant teenagers who say the classes give them reassurance and determination to be good mothers – especially as overwhelming negative messages they are bombarded with suggest the opposite.

> **Teenage pregnancy is not a cause of poverty, but often a symptom. For some young women, motherhood can seem like an escape**

However, a heavy-handed approach which forces, rather than offers teenage mums this kind of support is, in our experience, almost certain to provoke resentment from those young women who are already marginalised and deeply mistrustful of authority. YWCA supports the notion of a tailored, individualised and sustained process of support for those most in need as outlined by Prime Minister Tony Blair in his speech of September 5th on social exclusion to the Joseph Rowntree Foundation as opposed to an approach which makes blanket assumptions about teenage mothers and their children.

The labelling of all teenage parents and their children as a social problem and the growing tendency to use them as a scapegoat for the phenomenon of anti-social behaviour risks isolating them further and discouraging them from accessing the very public services they can benefit

from. It is difficult to imagine these women entering meaningfully into a process in which they believe their children have already been branded as future trouble-makers. In fact, the vast majority of young mums who come to YWCA say that the emotional impact of coping with public hostility and assumptions of their ability to be good parents is more difficult to cope with than the physical challenges they face.

Teenage pregnancy is not a cause of poverty, but often a symptom. For some young women, motherhood can seem like an escape from the prospect of an empty future and provide the status that enables them to re-insert themselves into their community. Contrary to the widely held myth that teenage pregnancy is a calculated choice to enable young

women to live off benefits, it can also provide many young women with the motivation to get back into education and employment to give themselves and their child a better life.

YWCA supports the proposal of stepping up sexual health advice to enable young women to make informed choices about their future. However, teenage pregnancy is not exclusively a result of ignorance about reproductive health. Sexual health advice must sit along with the provision of the infrastructure, economic security and aspirational vision to help a young woman thrive. Otherwise pregnancy will continue to remain the only meaningful option for many teenagers. In the meantime, teenage mums need support and encouragement, not blame and chastisement. The same goes for their children.

5 September 2006

⇨ The above information is reprinted with kind permission from the YWCA. Visit www.ywca.org.uk for more information.

The stigma of being a teenage mum

Hannah White gave birth to a baby in the middle of her GCSEs – and still got 12, seven of them As. She talks to Decca Aitkenhead about a broken condom, tough decisions, and the stigma of being a teenage mum

Hannah White answers the door, bleary-eyed in her pyjamas. It's 7am, two hours before the college day begins, and Hannah is padding round the small Blackpool flat she shares with her 19-year-old boyfriend, Jimmy Welsh, preparing bottles and looking for school books. Ebony, she laughs softly, will sleep until after nine unless she is woken, so Hannah teases her from the crib to be fed by Jimmy, while she fixes her hair in a mirror propped on the banisters in the hallway. The flat's overall aesthetic is more sixth-form common room than Mothercare, but among the CDs and books Ebony is carefully dressed and cuddled, her parents sleepy but purposeful and calm. Hannah walks her round the corner to a childminder, kisses her goodbye, and blends seamlessly into the teenage tide of baggy jeans and trainers making its way up the road to school.

Halfway through her GCSEs in May, Hannah gave birth to a 3.6kg (7lb 15oz) baby. She sat one of her papers 11 hours later, while still in hospital, and took the rest in a centre for teen mothers, listening to her baby's cries from an adjacent room. She is not the only GCSE student to have given birth this summer, but when the exam results were announced she certainly became one of the most surprising. She scored seven As, one of them starred, two Bs and a C, bringing her total – having sat two the previous year – to 12. She has just enrolled at sixth-form college, to study five A-levels.

'I didn't think I was capable of carrying a baby, I still felt like a child'

Hannah and Jimmy had been together for six months last September when she discovered she was pregnant. 'We'd done normal teenage things all summer,' she smiles. 'Gone to the pleasure beach, hung out like normal teenagers. It was brill, just ace. It was the time of my life.' Three weeks after a condom had broken the pair were in town and 'on the spur of the moment', they bought a pregnancy test.

'I looked at it and I just couldn't believe it. Part of me was like, I'm carrying a baby. But I didn't think I was capable of carrying a baby, I still felt like a child. But Jimmy was really positive. He was just really positive.' Hannah's mother and stepfather were less so, though, and for a month the family was in turmoil while Hannah 'walked around like a zombie', unsure what to do.

'We got given this virtual baby by a health visitor,' she laughs. 'We both hated that baby! God, we hated it. Compared to that baby Ebony's a doddle. I think it was meant to put you off – but I'm stubborn.'

By any standards, Hannah is an unusually intelligent and stable teenager. She had everything ahead of her. Why didn't she have a termination?

'It was just my gut instinct,' she says simply. 'It's not that I don't agree with people having abortions, but for me, I couldn't get rid of a baby. I didn't want a baby. I just wanted to keep the baby I had.'

At the First Steps centre in Blackpool for teenage mothers, Hannah was told she would be able to sit her GCSEs there. The centre helped the couple apply for housing benefit, and told them about Care To Learn – a government scheme that funds childcare for 13-19-year-old mothers who want to stay in education. The couple found a flat, Hannah's parents acted as guarantor, and three months before the birth the teenagers set up home together.

'It was a bit hectic,' Hannah says ruefully. 'Learning about bills and rent and all that. We'd never done it before. I'd never even done the washing before. My mum had to teach me how to work a washing machine. I'd never cooked a thing either; my mum had to teach me that too.'

Hannah's mother owns a small hotel in Blackpool. Paula Chew is only 41 herself, lively and brisk, and she admits that at first she didn't believe her daughter could become a mother without ruining her chances in life. Paula teeters on tears at times as she describes the last year, but it seems to be more from pride now than distress.

'It was difficult, telling my own parents,' she says. 'My grandma's still alive – but even she was just, oh well, Hannah isn't the first and she won't be the last. I think really everybody thought, my God, if it can happen to Hannah then it could happen to anyone. Hannah's not stupid, but these things happen.'

But Paula recalls visiting a chemist with her daughter in school uniform, and seeing how badly she was treated by the assistant. 'I said to Hannah, do you get that a lot? She said yeah, you do get that quite a lot. She'd never even complained about it to me. And it made me feel so upset for her. I thought, they don't know her! How can they judge my daughter when they don't know her? That's when I realised just what a bad press teenage mums get.'

Hannah brushes it off as 'just comments and looks, that's all'. What did hurt her, though, she says shyly, was the universal presumption of commiseration among people she knew. 'When I told people I was pregnant they'd always say, Oh! Are you keeping it? Ebony was never a baby, she was always an it. There was no, Oh how great! You're pregnant. It sounds awful, because I shouldn't expect it, but there does come a point when you want it, you want congratulation, you can't help wanting the same thing people 10 years older than me would get.'

Hannah comes from a close middle-class family; her stepfather works at Lancaster University, and she had been a studious teenager, quietly academic and dependable. Did she feel any sense of shame to find herself at a centre for teenage mothers, with all its social implications of failure? She nods.

'I thought, I can't believe I've ended up here with girls like this. But then, when I got talking to them, I realised they were nothing like the stereotype of teen mums either. Just really ordinary girls with ordinary lives. And some of them had managed to deal with an awful lot more than me.

'People are definitely more accepting towards me since my GCSE results, definitely. And you know, for myself, too, the GCSEs made me feel so much more confident – because it makes me feel not ashamed to say I'm a mum any more. I've proved it now, so I've got nothing left to prove. I just wanted to prove everyone wrong. I couldn't face the idea of being a failure.'

'Ebony was never a baby, she was always an it'

At half past four, Hannah gets back from college to collect her daughter. Her face is luminous with anticipation as she scoops her up. Our photographer is waiting to take pictures, but Ebony is crying with wind – and suddenly I realise we are all standing around staring at Hannah try to soothe her daughter. It would be an exposing moment for any young mother, but she is completely unselfconscious. Absorbed in her daughter, her self-possession is breathtaking.

Back at home, her boyfriend Jimmy is waiting for them. Though older than Hannah, he seems much younger; he has never seen a copy of the *Guardian*, thinks news is 'pants', and admits, 'I never thought I'd have my own kids. I always thought I'd be like this guy who goes out drinking and just messes about with his mates. That's all I thought I'd be doing.' Spinal problems have meant he cannot currently work, and he has the absent-minded dreaminess of a typical teenage boy. But he resents the assumption that he would even have considered abandoning Hannah, and his stoicism is manifestly soothing to her.

'The first couple of weeks were pretty hard, yeah. Hannah couldn't cope, she was getting stressed, crying her eyes out in the bedroom. We kept saying to each other, everything's going to be OK, right? And I'm

like, I don't know. I just get on with it really. That's all it is. Getting on with it.'

Later that night, Hannah's best friend Storm drops by to do homework. There are squeals over flirtatious emails a boy has sent her; Jimmy plays rock music; there is talk of a concert. Through the normal teenage rhythms of the evening, though, the centre of attention is always Ebony, and what had looked so incongruous to me that morning – a baby amid the paraphernalia of teenage life – is by now looking startlingly natural. Having had no previous life together, Hannah and Jimmy have nothing to be turned upside down.

After Ebony is in bed at 9.30, Hannah does half an hour of homework and half an hour of housework. White with exhaustion, she is still cheerful. 'It is a bit surreal. My friends are all talking about pocket money and stuff, and I feel like I'm living this secret life that no one understands. But when I've got my A-levels I'm going to get a job, and I won't be on benefits any more. I've got a lot to be thankful for.'

First published in the Guardian, *17 September 2005*

© Decca Aitkenhead

Getting teenage mums 'back to school'

New research identifies the best ways to re-engage the disengaged and break the cycle of underachievement

Pregnancy can provide a spur for many previously under-achieving young mums to improve their basic skills in reading, writing and mathematics and make a successful transition back into education – if the right combination of educational provision and practical support is available – according to *Raising Expectations*, a new book from the Basic Skills Agency on Monday 29th May.

In a recent report on school-age mums-to-be less than half were attending school regularly when they became pregnant

Research shows that under-achievers are more likely to become teenage parents (in a recent report on school-age mums-to-be less than half were attending school regularly when they became pregnant – Universities of Bristol and Newcastle, 2005). Their children are also likely to continue the pattern of under-achievement.

Using case studies with learners and teachers in a range of non-school settings, *Raising Expectations* (and a complementary suite of materials for teachers) illustrates how the cycle can be stopped. The book highlights a number of keys to success, including: motivating and raising the aspirations of disengaged young people – an area in which out-of-school units are particularly successful; providing a broad curriculum; and offering programmes in parenting and personal development alongside

GCSEs and NVQs. Other keys to success are: ensuring that teenage parents achieve accreditation before they leave specialist provision – to help them continue their studies; and embedding basic skills learning within other programmes to make sure young parents have the literacy, language and numeracy skills they need.

In addition *Raising Expectations* highlights the importance of providing childcare on-site and help with travel costs and illustrates the need for good links and strong communication between referral agencies and support networks – to encourage learners to progress to further training.

Whilst recognising the successes of the Government's 10-year National Teenage Pregnancy Strategy (launched in 1999), *Raising Expectations* also identifies a number of barriers which may impact on the Strategy's success in getting teenage parents back into education. These include the difficulty of engaging teenage fathers; practical financial issues, pressures to move young people into work too quickly; and some younger parents' lack of basic skills, confidence and self-esteem.
29 May 2006

⇨ The above information is reprinted with kind permission from the Basic Skills Agency. Visit www.basic-skills.co.uk for more information.

When lads become dads

We regard them as so feckless, expect so little of them, that we don't even know how many teenage fathers there are in Britain. Yvonne Roberts meets three

Daniel Cole knew his girlfriend, Kim, was pregnant when she woke up feeling sick for a couple of days. 'The doctor couldn't find anything wrong. Then it clicked. I knew she had to do the test in the morning when the pee is fresh. That's the only thing I remember from sex education at school.'

Daniel was 19, Kim 17. 'We didn't use contraception because condoms are too expensive and I didn't know where to get them for free. As I see it, if you are man enough to have sex you should be man enough to live with the consequences ...'

Daniel's mother was 'over the moon' at the news, Kim's wasn't. 'Not happy at all,' Daniel smiles wryly. 'She said I had no job and no education; she wanted us to get rid of it. She gave me grief for eight and a half months. Now, we get on fine.'

As Daniel talks, Tyler, now 18 months old, sits contentedly on his dad's lap, immaculate in designer gear. 'I was there at the birth. I cut the cord. I used to feed and change my brothers and sisters, so I've always done that with Tyler. Only thing I can't do is get up to him in the night when he and Kim stay with me – and that winds Kim up ...'

Kim, who lives with her mum, receives £85 a week for herself and the baby. Daniel, who has a flat and who sees Kim and Tyler every day, receives £185 a fortnight, including incapacity benefit.

'I help her, she helps me, because that's helping Tyler. Every time I get paid, I buy something new for him. The other day the sole came off my trainers but now, I put my son before myself, I've got to dress him smart. See that dummy,' Daniel adds, '£3.75 a time and he kept losing it. So I bought a solid gold £75 chain to put it on and they don't get lost any more.'

No one knows precisely how many teenage fathers there are in the UK. The Social Exclusion Report on Teenage Pregnancy, published several years ago, barely gave fathers a mention. What is known is that, in 2004, 56,000 babies were born to teenage girls.

Young fathers often have to prove to sceptical adults, such as health visitors, that male and teenage doesn't automatically add up to useless. Thousands of young men are desperately trying to sustain relationships with their children, against the grain of everyone else's expectations.

Daniel is one of six. Two of his brothers are autistic. His mother had him when she was in care, aged 15. Daniel has never known his father and a stepfather left a while ago. Small and wiry, he was bullied and fought back. Deemed out of control, he was sent to a local authority boarding school. At 15, when his schooling ended, he was unable to read or write.

Young fathers often have to prove to sceptical adults, such as health visitors, that male and teenage doesn't automatically add up to useless

---

'I'm looking for the key to open my brain,' he says smiling. 'I always say my mum left it at the hospital when she had me. People have said to me about Tyler, "You're dyslexic, how are you going to bring this kid up?" I said it's not just about reading, it's about what's in your heart and the love that you give him.

'When he's older I'll have to explain, "If you want to read you'll have to go to your mum." Kim's all right, man. She's really clever. She's going back to college when she's older. People call me mongol,' Daniel adds, shrugging. 'I don't let it get to me.'

We talk in a room belonging to a charity, Free@Last, founded by the community worker John Street, in the deprived area of Nechells in Birmingham. Supporting fathers of all ages is one of its aims. 'We've

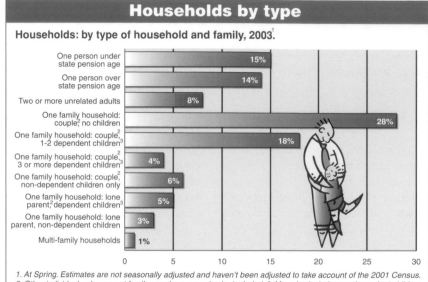
been telling Daniel for years about his talents,' John says. 'But he's had a lifetime of hearing he's no good. He is a fantastic dad and Kim and he make a good couple.'

'I want Tyler to get a job, get married, have a child in that order,' Daniel says. 'I don't want him to be a dole brain like me.'

According to research, if a father is present at the birth, and has his name on the birth certificate, the chances of remaining positively in the baby's life are vastly increased

---

Daniel is keen to become an electrician. 'I can fix anything,' he says. 'I've been to hospital loads of times, I've given myself that many shocks.' He even offered to serve an apprenticeship unpaid. 'They said no. It's my dyslexia and the paperwork.'

Managing anger, once Daniel's weakness, has become his forte since fatherhood. 'When Tyler is teething, if it's getting out of hand, I walk out of the room. It takes a man to do that. I used to lash out, get into fights, but I never show anger to my son or girlfriend.

'I'm bringing Tyler up the way my mum brought us up. If Tyler misbehaves, he'll have time out in his room, no smacking. We're lucky,' Daniel points out, 'we get a lot of support from our families.'

According to research, if a father is present at the birth, and has his name on the birth certificate, the chances of remaining positively in the baby's life are vastly increased. When I first meet Dean Gray, 17, he had been a father for five days but had yet to see his daughter, Tiffany. Tiffany's mother, Dean's ex-girlfriend, Nicola, is also 17. 'I don't feel like a dad,' Dean says. 'I think there's a list of importance in who sees the baby. The mother pops it out. She sees it first, then the dad, then their parents ... but not me. I'm at the bottom of the list.'

Dean is mad about cars. He steals them, drives them away and then sets fire to them. He also self-harms when drunk and has been arrested several times for assault. He's been repeatedly warned for threatening Nicola.

'When I heard she was pregnant, I told the police everything I'd done ready for the baby. I got a two-year driving ban and a 12-month referral order. Then, one night, there's a knock at the door and it's the police. Normally, I'd run. But I said to myself, No, I'm clean. But Nicola had complained I'd

been harassing her by text. I was put in a cell and cried all night.'

Sian Williams is a passionately committed young fathers' worker in Northampton, trying to help teenagers such as Dean. She says that some teenage mothers can be devious. They tell the dads they're not allowed at the scan or the birth, depending on their mood and they ration time with the baby in return for gifts. On this occasion, she says Nicola's family is right to be concerned about Dean's behaviour. For several days the youth offending team negotiate, on Dean's behalf, so he can see his daughter. 'I've been out of trouble for two months,' he protests. 'That's really good for me.'

A week later, father and daughter meet under supervision. She has black hair and looks just like Dean. 'She's all right,' he says. A month later, he is still seeing his daughter regularly, but he has been in trouble again. 'I do feel more like a dad. I am trying because of the baby. But it is hard.'

John Dunlop, 17, has a daughter, Sian-Leigh, aged one, with Vicki, aged 16. He is very determined to be the best kind of father – unlike his own. 'We met when Vicki were 13,' John says, talking near the YMCA where he now lives. His arms are bruised. Mementos of being removed, drunk, from a local pub by a bouncer 'Like an old married couple we were.

She dropped out of school because of me and I dropped out of school because of her. Then we got engaged and it was hell. But we got through it.'

Vicki was 15 when she miscarried. Then, she became pregnant again. 'We knew we were right for each other so we planned the second time. I was at the birth. It was a caesarean and my name's on the certificate,' John says proudly.

His resilience is like a live current. He says his mother chucked him out when he was nine, 'I reminded her too much of my dad and he's an arsehole – a thief and a wife-beater. He said he'd come on a Saturday to take me to McDonald's. He never came. My mum used to say I was rubbish just like him.'

Sian Williams says that 'the first thing I try to do with our young dads is encourage them to like themselves. If they don't like themselves, how can they love a baby?'

The importance of a 'trusted adult', supporting young parents, was underlined in the social exclusion report. Sian, however, is only funded for a year. 'We've got dozens of young dads,' she says. 'Some have fended for themselves on the streets since they were young. We do what we can. Sometimes, that means just buying them a bag of chips, having a chat and saying, "You're doing all right, mate."

'Often, when a girlfriend says she's pregnant, they don't realise how much they will love that child – and how difficult it will be to stay in that baby's life. Some fight so hard, they are positively heroic.'

John lived with his grandad, then he was fostered and later moved in with Vicki's family. 'I get on brilliant with her mum.' Now, his relationship is in tricky waters, 'Vicki wants me to be somebody I'm not.' He is anxious to ensure access to Sian-Leigh. 'I try and see her every day, even if Vicki and me aren't together, Sian has my heart.'

John is on a Prince's Trust training course, laying bricks, the latest of several courses. He receives £129 a fortnight – £40 goes to the YMCA in rent and he is paying off arrears. 'I don't eat much. I spend my money on DVDs and stuff for Vicki and the baby. Being a dad is the best thing that's happened to me,' he adds. 'I said "Dadadada" to Sian-Leigh for months and when she finally did say "Dada", that were bloody brilliant.'
10 June 2006

Toddlers to help halt teen pregnancies

By Gaby Hinsliff, Political Editor

Schoolgirls at risk of pregnancy could be sent on a programme that uses babies to put them off premature parenthood, under new government plans to tackle teenage conception.

The move follows promising results from a pioneering project in London that allows teenagers to look after young children in a nursery, so learning at first hand how tiring and time-consuming parenthood can be.

Hilary Armstrong, who was appointed cabinet minister for social justice in last Friday's reshuffle, visited the Teens to Toddlers project yesterday and said she would now consider spreading such programmes across the country.

'These young adolescents are learning so much about themselves and their own capabilities – as well as how difficult it is to have young children,' she said.

'It's a combination of working with a child in a nursery on a regular basis but also sessions where they talk through relationships, how they see child rearing or parenting skills. It affects their self esteem, but it also benefits the children.'

While ordinarily about 10 of the group would have been expected to get pregnant during the lifetime of the programme, none so far had, she said.

Armstrong said she would concentrate on early intervention with problem families, linking it to the government's drive against antisocial behaviour. Teenage pregnancy rates have fallen in recent years overall, but progress remains patchy across the country, with some boroughs showing inexplicable rises. The Prime Minister's strategy unit has been carrying out an analysis of what factors are most likely to stop schoolgirls conceiving.

Armstrong's brief is to focus on teenage pregnancies and children in care, as well as the mentally ill, for whom she said the criminal justice system had too often been a 'safety net' that did not work.
7 May 2006

Welfare and single parenthood in the UK

This ESRC information provides a statistical overview of welfare and single parenthood in the UK

Lone parents in the UK

There are 1.8 million one-parent families in Britain and they care for nearly 3 million children. About nine out of ten lone parents are women. The median age for a lone parent is 35, and at any one time only 3 per cent of lone mothers are teenagers.

Lone parenthood is now often a stage in the life-cycle, lasting on average around five years. Lone parents from black or minority ethnic communities make up 12 per cent of all lone parents compared to 7.9 per cent of the UK's population.

Children in one-parent families

In 2004, one in four dependent children lived in one-parent families. This was an increase from 1 in 14 in 1972. The bar chart on page 29 shows the number of dependent children by family type in the UK.

While one-third of lone mothers have a child under five, children in families headed by lone fathers tended to be older than children in other types of families. In 2001, the youngest child in nearly half of lone-father families was aged over 11.

Teenage single mothers

Despite media headlines suggesting otherwise, overall, teenage pregnancies have fallen nationally by 9.4 per cent since 1999. In 1970, young women aged 15 to 19 in England and Wales were almost twice as likely to become mothers as they are today. Furthermore, the belief held in some circles that teenagers only get pregnant to get a council house is not backed by facts. Seven out of ten 15- and 16-year-old mothers, and around half of 17- and 18-year-old mothers, stay in the family home.

One-parent families: income and welfare benefits

Forty-two per cent of all poor children live in one-parent families. One-third (33 per cent) of one-parent families live on gross incomes of £200 a week or less. This compares with 3 per cent of married couples, and 10 per cent of cohabiting couples.

Today, 55 per cent of lone parents are in work

One-parent families: employment and welfare benefits

Research from the Joseph Rowntree Foundation during the 1990s showed that most lone mothers actively look for work to escape from benefit. A study of 6,700 lone mothers claiming Income Support found that only one in five was receiving the benefit throughout a four-year period from 1993 to 1997. Other investigations highlight a lack of qualifications and the high cost of childcare in the UK as reasons preventing lone mothers returning to work.

Today 55 per cent of lone parents are in work, a rise of 44 per cent from 1997. Research from the Institute for Fiscal Studies suggests part of this increase is because of the new Working Families' Tax Credit which replaced Family Credit in 1999. It estimates that the new tax credit increased the numbers of lone mothers who worked by just over 5 per cent by 2002.

Further research from the Institute for Social and Economic Research supports this. By May 2000, the new Working Families' Tax Credit was being claimed by 30 per cent more lone parents than those who claimed its predecessor. By the end of 2001, an additional 135,000 lone mothers were in eligible employment. More than 50 per cent of this increase was attributable to lone mothers who took advantage of the generous childcare tax credit component and could then pay for childcare.

However, these tax credits have been strongly criticised. Evidence from 150,000 cases dealt with by the Citizens' Advice Bureau in 2004-05 highlighted a high level of error in administering the tax credits which has caused a third of claimants to be overpaid and subsequently pushed into poverty when asked to repay. The table on page 29 demonstrates five of these cases.

And finally...

The ESRC Research Group on Care, Values and the Future of Welfare (CAVA) reasons that the growth of single parenthood is just one example of the many ways in which family life in Britain is changing, and it argues that social policy needs to change to be more in line with the way we live.

⇨ The above information is re-printed with kind permission from the Economic and Social Research Council. Visit www.esrc.ac.uk for more information.

© ESRC

Statistics taken from the ESRC factsheet *Welfare and Single Parenthood in the UK*

Number of dependent children by family type, 2004, UK

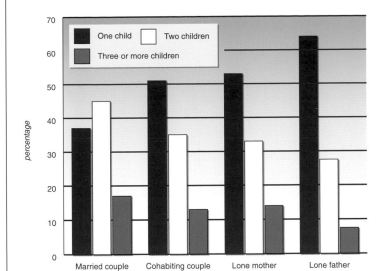

Source: Office for National Statistics. Crown copyright.

Dependent children by family type, 2004, UK

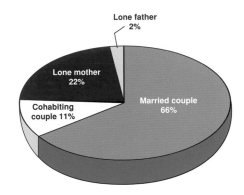

Source: Office for National Statistics (data from the 2001 Census. Crown copyright.

Income support claimants by statistical group: 1997 to 2005

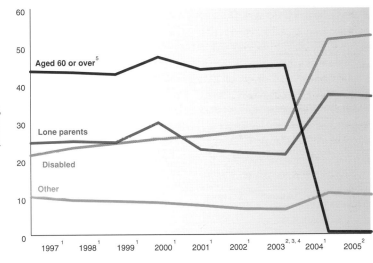

1. Figures produced by calculating mean average for February, May, August and November figures.
2. February figures only.
3. New tax credits were introduced in April 2003 and may affect figures.
4. Claimants aged 60 and over transferred to Pension Credit on 6 October 2003.
5. Includes claimants aged under 60 where there is a partner aged 60 or over.

Source: Department for Work and Pensions. Crown copyright.

Cases of lone parents who had to repay overpayments of child tax credit

Family composition	Total income inc. child tax credit £	CTC lost £	% CTC reduction	New weekly income £
Lone parent 3 children	£185.90 (CTC £93.70)	£86.73	93%	£99.17
Lone parent 2 children	£147.40 (CTC £65.95)	£30.70	47%	£116.70
Lone parent 1 child	£108.90 (CTC £38.20)	£32.87	86%	£76.03
Lone parent 1 child	£108.90 (CTC £38.20)	£35.17	92%	£73.73
Lone parent 1 child	£108.90 (CTC £38.20)	£24.90	65%	£84.00

Source: Citizen's Advice Bureau.

Lone parent families

Action facts

Lone parents and their children now make up an important section of our society. Policies aimed at them will have a significant social effect.

How many lone-parent families are there?

⇨ Between 1996 and 2004, the number of lone-mother families increased by 12% to 2.3 million.

⇨ In 2004 nine out of ten lone parents were lone mothers.
(Statistics taken fron ONS.)

Between 1996 and 2004, the number of lone-mother families increased by 12% to 2.3 million

---

⇨ Between 2003 and 2004, the percentage of lone-parent households (with one child) was ten times less likely to be on the £500-£600 (a week) income bracket than a two-parent household with one child.

⇨ The highest percentage of income for lone parents was between £100 and £200 per week. Whereas for two-parent households it was between £800 and £900 per week (both with 1 child).
(Statistics taken from DWP.)

⇨ Labour Force Survey estimates for spring 2005 show the employment rate for lone parents was 56.2%. This is an increase of 5.2% since 2000.
(Statistics taken from ONS.)

⇨ The UK average of lone-parent families is 25.58%.

⇨ The highest proportion of lone-parent families is in Lambeth in London. Where 48% of families with dependent children are lone-parent families. The lowest proportion of lone-parent families was in the South East

GINGERBREAD
the organisation for lone parent families

(Wokingham, Chiltern, South Buckinghamshire and Hart) with a percentage of just 13%.
(Statistics taken from ONS.)

⇨ The percentage of lone mothers who are economically active has increased from 48% in 1992 to 57% in 2002. With 23% working full-time and 28% part-time. Compared with 31% who stay at home to look after family/home.
(Labour Force Survey, ONS. Available online at: http://www.statistics.gov.uk/statbase/expodata/spreadsheets/d6253.xls)

⇨ Nearly 2 million tax credits were overpaid in the tax year 2003-2004. Out of those, 353,000 were to lone parents. The large majority of these overpayments have been made because of serious flaws in the Revenues and Customs systems. With no limit on the amount of tax credit presently, the amount lone families are left with, while paying back overpayments is well below the Income Support or breadline level.
(One Parent Families.)

⇨ The CSA has had endless problems since its launch in 1993:

⇨ In 2001, the CSA was owed more than £1 billion in maintenance payments, and had written off two-thirds as it was uncollectable.

⇨ In 2003 the new computer and phone system was launched. The system was flawed and technical problems led to only 4% of the 150,000 new claimants receiving a payment.

⇨ In 2004 the unprocessed claims reached 170,00, with 75,000

being lost in the new IT system. The backlog was rising by 30,000 every 3 months.
(The *Guardian*, 12/04/05, 'Timeline: the CSA crisis' available online from: http://society.guardian.co.uk/children/story/0,1074,1457948,00.html)

⇨ The amount of maintenance collected by the CSA has fallen by 2% in real terms.

⇨ The proportion of lone parents receiving a first payment has fallen by a third.

⇨ The backlog of lone parents waiting for an assessment has increased by 20%.
(The *Guardian*, 08/09/05, 'CSA is ignoring failures.' Available online from: http://society.guardian.co.uk/print/0,3858,5280362-110464,00.html)

⇨ More than a million phone calls in 2004/05 were abandoned as parents give up trying to get through to the CSA.

⇨ The proportion of lone parents receiving a first payment dropped from 72% to 52%.
(The *Guardian*, 10/09/05, 'Plight of single parents worsens.' Available online from http://society.guardian.co.uk/print/0,3858,5281767-110464,00.html.)

⇨ The above information is reprinted with kind permission from Gingerbread. Visit www.gingerbread.org.uk for more information.

© *Gingerbread*

Dependent children

1 in 4 in lone-parent families

In 2004 there were 7.4 million families with 13.1 million dependent children living in them in the UK. Most of these children (66 per cent) lived in a married couple family.

One in four dependent children lived in a lone-parent family in 2004. This was an increase from 1 in 14 in 1972.

The average number of children in a family declined from 2.0 in 1971 to 1.8 in 2004. Married couple families were generally larger than other family types, with an average 1.8 children in 2004, compared with 1.7 in cohabiting couple and lone-mother families.

In 2004 there were 7.4 million families with 13.1 million dependent children living in them in the UK. Most of these children (66 per cent) lived in a married couple family

---

In 2004 nearly two-thirds (64 per cent) of lone-father families had only one child living with them, the largest proportion of any family type. The proportion of married couple families with one child was the smallest at 37 per cent. Married couples were more likely than other family types to have three or more children.

Children in families headed by lone fathers tended to be older than children in other types of families. In 2001 the youngest child in nearly half of lone-father families was aged over 11. This compared with around a quarter of married couple and lone-mother families, and a seventh of cohabiting couple families. This pattern reflects cohabiting couple families and lone mothers being

generally younger than married couple families and lone fathers.

Some children live in different family types during their childhood, this is a result of changes in relationship and childbearing patterns, such as the rise in births outside marriage and the growth in divorce and cohabitation.

Children can be affected by the breakdown of marriage and cohabiting unions and/or the creation of new partnerships. In 2003, 153,500 children under 16 were affected by their parents divorcing in England and Wales, just over one in five were under five years old.

One in four women who gave birth outside marriage in 1988 went on to marry in the subsequent eight years, most of them married the child's father.

Some children do not live in families at all. In 2001, 139,000 children were living in other households in the UK, this includes living with adults or other relatives who are not their parents. An additional 52,000 children under 16 lived in communal establishments such as a children's home.

Sources
⇨ Census, 2001, Office for National Statistics; General Register Office for Scotland; Northern Ireland Statistics and Research Agency
⇨ Labour Force Survey, spring 2004, Office for National Statistics
⇨ General Household Survey, 1971 and 1972, Office for National Statistics
⇨ Children of divorced couples: Office for National Statistics

Notes
⇨ Household: a person living alone, or a group of people living at the same address who have the address as their only or main residence and either share one main meal a day or share the living accommodation (or both).
⇨ Family: a married/cohabiting couple with or without child(ren), or a lone parent with child(ren).
⇨ Dependent children: aged under 16, or aged 16-18 in full-time education and never married.

All data refer to dependent children except for children in communal establishments. In the Census, children not in a household are not classified as either dependent or non-dependent.

Published on 7 July 2005

⇨ The above information is reprinted with kind permission from the Office for National Statistics. Please visit their website at www.statistics.gov.uk for more information.

© Crown copyright

Why UK is Europe's single-parent capital

Generous benefits for lone mothers have made Britain the single-parent capital of Europe, according to research.

It has the highest number of single-parent families and pays them almost the highest level of state handouts.

Researchers found the two factors were linked – and said that every £690 increase in payments makes it 3.5 per cent more likely a woman will become a lone mother.

Critics warn that children from lone-mother households are far more likely than those from stable married families to do badly at school and to suffer ill health

---

The study provides powerful evidence that Labour's flagship tax credit system, which pours billions into payments for lone mothers, undermines family life.

Critics warn that children from lone-mother households are far more likely than those from stable married families to do badly at school and to suffer ill health.

They are also more likely to become unemployed or find only poor-paying jobs, to fall into drug use or crime, and to become single parents themselves.

The study by Dr Libertad Gonzalez of the Pompeu Fabra University in Barcelona found that eight per cent of British women aged between 18 and 35 are bringing up children on their own.

That proportion is nearly four times the level in France, more than twice the rate in Germany and double

By Steve Doughty, Social Affairs Correspondent

the rate in Holland.

The one in four single parents most dependent on benefits received more than £6,400 in 2001 – higher than in any other European country except Holland.

British benefit levels were nearly double those paid in Germany and nearly three times those paid in France. They were also double the amount paid to UK parents in similar circumstances in 1994.

Dr Gonzalez said that Britain, Germany and Ireland saw the biggest leap in these benefits during the late 1990s.

Using figures from all EU countries, she calculated that each increase of 1,000 euros – about £690 – in benefits means a 3.5 per cent increase in the likelihood of a woman becoming a single mother.

She said there were 'positive and significant' indications that 'countries where single mothers are more prevalent also provide higher benefit levels'.

And she found that the impact of benefits was greatest on young unmarried women rather than those contemplating breaking up two-parent families.

The findings underline concerns about the effects of the handouts, recognised by Tony Blair in the years after his 1997 election victory when Downing Street dropped hints that young single mothers might be required to live in hostels. Since then, however, more of the tax credits scheme – which costs taxpayers £20billion a year – has gone into payments and childcare for single mothers working more than 16 hours a week.

The system by which lone parents are given social housing almost automatically remains unchanged.

Critics of the tax credit system also maintain that by favouring lone parents over couple families, the benefits provide incentives for family break-up or for mothers to stay single.

Dr Gonzalez's findings, to be published next month at a European Union conference of academics, were based on EU programmes tracking the lives of thousands of people in each of the 14 European countries.

⇨ This article first appeared in the *Daily Mail*, 18 April 2006

© 2006 Associated Newspapers Ltd

How the benefits compare

Proportion of women aged 18 to 35 who are single mothers, 2001

Benefits paid to the most dependent single mothers, 2001

Country	Proportion	Benefits
UK	8%	£6,400
Ireland	4.5%	£5,587
Holland	3.9%	£6,860
Germany	3.5%	£3,400
Austria	3.4%	£2,879
Finland	2.8%	£3,959
Denmark	2.6%	£4,799
Belgium	2.5%	£3,274
France	2.2%	£2,349
Luxembourg	1.1%	£3,455
Spain	0.9%	£0
Greece	0.9%	£0
Portugal	0.6%	£539
Italy	0.4%	£0

Source: European Community Household Panel. Research by Dr Libertad Gonzalez, Pompeu Fabra University, Barcelona. Sourced from the Daily Mail, Why UK is Europe's single-parent capital.

Benefits and tax credits

Information for lone parents

This article is a basic guide to the main benefits and tax credits available to lone-parent families; it is not intended to be a statement of the law. There are a range of additional benefit payments made in certain circumstances such as during pregnancy or to those who are sick or disabled. It may be necessary to seek individual advice. See Further help below.

Child Tax Credit

Child Tax Credit is paid by the Tax Credit Office, which is part of Her Majesty's Revenue and Customs. It is paid in addition to Child Benefit whether parents are in or out of work. Claimants receiving Child Tax Credit as a couple, must inform the Tax Credit Office after separating from a spouse or partner or risk a financial penalty.

Lone parents who are receiving payments for their children as part of Income Support, or income-based Jobseeker's Allowance, who then claim Child Tax Credit, will not be better off as Child Tax Credit is counted as income, when Income Support is calculated.

For more information see Gingerbread fact sheet 17: *Introduction to Tax Credits*. If you are expecting a

GINGERBREAD
the organisation for lone parent families

baby, see Gingerbread fact sheet 1: *Maternity checklist*.

Income Support

Income Support can be claimed by lone parents who are not working or who work for less than 16 hours a week. Claims are made at Jobcentre Plus offices, see Further help.

⇨ To be eligible lone parents must be responsible for a child aged under 16, be a carer or be sick or disabled. Some pregnant women, young people aged between 16 and 18, people over the age of 50, those on training courses and the recently bereaved can also claim Income Support. If none of these apply, see Jobseeker's Allowance below.

⇨ To be eligible, capital including savings must be less than of £16,000 in total. Capital over £6,000 will affect the amount of Income Support that is paid.

⇨ The maximum amount payable is called the Applicable Amount. The adult personal allowance is £57.45 per week (April 2006) which is paid to most lone parents. Lower rates apply for parents under the age of 18. See Gingerbread fact sheet 8: *Benefits and support for pregnant teenagers and young mothers*.

⇨ Additional payments called Premiums are made in certain circumstances. These include Disability, Carer and Bereavement premium.

⇨ Some lone parents receive payments for their children and a Family Premium, but these were replaced with the payment of Child Tax Credit in 2003 for new claims. See Child Tax Credit above.

⇨ Once the Applicable Amount is calculated, other money coming in is usually deducted pound for pound. There are some excep-tions including for lone parents the first £20 a week of earnings. Jobcentre Plus need to be kept informed of any earnings and other income that is received. Child Benefit is no longer deducted, unless you are receiving allowances for your children in your Income Support. See Child Support Agency below for the rules about child maintenance.

Jobseeker's Allowance

Jobseeker's Allowance can be claimed by lone parents who are not working or who work less than 16 hours a week instead of Income Support. Claims are made at Jobcentre Plus offices, see Further help. Claimants must be capable of work (i.e. not too ill to work) and must demonstrate that they are 'available for work' and 'actively seeking work'. In addition claimants must attend a Jobseeker's interview and sign a Job Seeker's Agreement, which outlines the steps they will take to find work. Claimants also have to 'sign on' at least fortnightly in order to receive benefit.

The maximum amount paid is called the Applicable Amount. The adult personal allowance is £57.45 per week (April 2006) which is the same as Income Support. Lone parents can continue to receive Child Benefit and Child Tax Credit for their children until the age of 20 if their children meet the conditions. See Gingerbread fact sheet 9: *Financial support for young people*.

There are two kinds of Jobseeker's Allowance:

⇨ Contribution based – for those who have worked recently. It is based on National Insurance (NI) contributions. There is no capital limit and most income apart from pensions and most earnings are ignored. Claimants are not required to apply to the Child Support Agency. Lone parents with capital or income which reduces or disqualifies them from entitlement to Income Support may be eligible for contribution-based Jobseeker's Allowance instead. They will need to meet the qualifying conditions. Contribution-based Jobseeker's Allowance is only paid for up to 182 days (6 months) at any one time.

⇨ Income based – for lone parents that have not paid enough National Insurance contributions. This is means tested in a similar way to Income Support. Lone parents, whose youngest child is 16 or over, can claim Jobseeker's Allowance when they are no longer entitled to Income Support. Income-based Jobseeker's Allowance claimants are required to apply to the Child Support Agency, see below.

Lone parents with children under 16 that require help to find work; can join the New Deal for Lone Parents. See fact sheet 16: *The New Deal for Lone Parents*.

Help with housing costs through Income Support and income-based Jobseeker's Allowance

Income Support and income-based Jobseeker's Allowance include help with housing costs towards the cost of mortgage interest payments. There is no help towards the capital or any endowment policy linked to the mortgage. The payments can be made if an ex-partner is not paying, whether in joint names or his/her sole name.[1] There is a waiting period before payments are made. See Waiting periods below. Payments are then made directly to the lender, and only up to a standard interest rate which is set by the Department of Work and Pensions. This may be less than is due to be paid. In most circumstances the maximum loan taken into account is £100,000, so additional payments will not be made if the balance of the loan is higher.

Waiting periods
⇨ Mortgages taken out before 2 October 1995 – there is no help for the first 8 weeks of a claim, then half the interest for the next 18 weeks, and from week 19 onwards the maximum allowable payment will be made.
⇨ Mortgages taken out on or after 2 October 1995 – the waiting period is 39 weeks, after which the maximum allowable payment will be made. Lone parents that have been abandoned[2] by a partner who have at least one child under 16, should only wait for the shorter period as above, if they have been 'constructively abandoned'. This means the behaviour of their partner was such as to give you little reasonable option but to leave him/her.[3]

Income Support can be claimed by lone parents who are not working or who work for less than 16 hours a week

---

Income Support and income-based Jobseeker's Allowance claimants are entitled to free prescriptions, dental treatment, eye tests and travel to hospital for treatment. Their children qualify for free school meals.

Child Support Agency

When lone parents claim Income Support and income-based Jobseeker's Allowance, the benefit claim is treated as an application for child maintenance to the Child Support Agency. The Child Support Agency will require information in order to trace the other parent, calculate and collect child maintenance from them unless the parent opts out, see below.

Since 3 March 2003 new benefit claimants are able to keep up to £10 a week in child maintenance before benefit payment is reduced. This is called the Child Maintenance Premium. See Gingerbread fact sheet 7: *The Child Support Agency*.

Lone parents with 'old rules' Child Support Agency cases (pre March 2003) do not receive the Child Maintenance Premium so any maintenance received directly by the parent or collected by the Child Support Agency will reduce benefit payments.

Opting out
Lone parents can indicate they wish to opt out on the Income Support and income-based Jobseeker's Allowance claim form or at any time by contacting Jobcentre Plus. If a parent chooses to opt out, they will usually be interviewed by Jobcentre Plus to find out the reasons for doing so.

If a parent believes they or their children will be at risk of harm or undue distress by making an application for maintenance, the interview is their opportunity to demonstrate this. This is called Good Cause. If Good Cause is accepted, then a parent does not need to co-operate with the Child Support Agency and apply for maintenance. If a parent fails to provide reasons for opting out or their reasons are not considered Good Cause by Jobcentre Plus, a Jobcentre Plus decision maker can impose a penalty. The penalty or Reduced Benefit Direction can reduce the weekly personal allowance by up to 40% (currently £22.98 a week). Jobcentre Plus cannot impose the penalty if the parent is receiving the disability premium or a higher pensioner premium as part of their benefit, see above.

Housing Benefit and Council Tax

Income Support or income-based Jobseeker's Allowance claimants living in rented accommodation, will usually be entitled to Housing Benefit. In some areas there will be a Local Housing Allowance instead. There is a short claim form included in the Income Support and income-based Jobseeker's Allowance claim packs. Housing Benefit is administered and paid by the local authority. Lone parents should contact the local authority and inform them that you have made a claim for Income Support or income-based Jobseeker's Allowance. The local authority will then issue a more detailed claim form. Council tenants usually receive benefit that covers all the rent apart from extras such as fuel charges. For private or Housing Association tenants, there may be a restriction on the level of Housing Benefit if the local rent officer decides that the accommodation is too large or the rent is too high for the area.

Income Support and income-based Jobseeker's Allowance claimants are also entitled to full Council Tax Benefit. A claim for Council Tax Benefit should be made at the same time as Housing Benefit. If the lone parent is the only person in the household aged over 18 (full-time students are 'invisible' for council tax purposes) they will be entitled to a Single Adult Discount of 25% off their council tax bill, regardless of their income.

Lone parents who are not entitled to Income Support or income-based Jobseeker's Allowance may still qualify for Housing Benefit and/or Council Tax Benefit. See Gingerbread fact sheets 21: *Help with your rent* and fact sheet 22: *Help with your Council Tax*.

Working Tax Credit

Lone parents that work for an average of at least 16 hours a week, or are on Maternity Leave from a job of at least 16 hours a week, may be entitled to Working Tax Credit. Claims for tax credits are made to the Tax Credit Office which is part of Her Majesty's Revenue and Customs. See Further help.

⇨ Working Tax Credit calculations are usually based on annual income from a previous tax year.
⇨ The amount is calculated by adding together a basic element, lone-parent element and child-care element, which is up to 80% of eligible childcare costs for children under 15 (16 if disabled) up to a set limit. Eligible childcare includes OFSTED registered and providers approved under the Childcare Approval Scheme or the National Care Standards Inspectorate for Wales.
⇨ Additional elements are added to the calculation in certain circumstances and include the disability element, 30-hour element and 50-plus element.
⇨ This gives a maximum Working

Tax Credit figure. If gross taxable income in 2005/6 was £5,220 or less, the entitlement is the maximum amount. If gross income is more than £5,220, Working Tax Credit entitlement is reduced by 37p for every extra pound.
⇨ The Working Tax Credit calculation ignores Income Support and income-based Jobseeker's Allowance, Child Benefit and any child or spousal maintenance income.

⇨ Lone parents are not required to co-operate with the Child Support Agency when claiming tax credits.

For more information see Gingerbread fact sheet 17: *Introduction to Tax Credits*.

Other help

Lone parents on a low income (including Working Tax claimants) may be eligible for free prescriptions and health benefits. An exemption card is issued to parents that qualify. Others may still be able to get some help with the costs, applications are made on form HC1, available from Jobcentre Plus or the Post Office.

The children of lone parents receiving Working Tax Credit do not qualify for free school meals.

There is no help towards mortgage interest payments for Working Tax Credit claimants but lone parents in rented accommodation may still qualify for Housing Benefit and owner occupiers and tenants may qualify for a small amount of Council

Tax Benefit and/or the Single Adult Discount.

See Gingerbread fact sheet 21: *Help with your rent* and fact sheet 22: *Help with your Council Tax*.

Further help
Gingerbread Advice Line
0800 018 4318
www.gingerbread.org.uk
One Parent Families Lone Parent Helpline
0800 018 5026
www.oneparentfamilies.org.uk
Jobcentre Plus
www.jobcentreplus.gov.uk
Tax Credits Enquiry Line
0845 300 3900
www.hmrc.gov.uk
Child Benefit Centre
0845 302 1444
www.hmrc.gov.uk
Child Support Agency
08457 133 133
www.csa.gov.uk

Notes
1 This is according to a Social Security Commissioner's decision no. SCB/213/1987. You may need to quote this if the BA says you cannot get help with mortgage interest.
2 Commissioner's decision CIS/5177/1997 said that abandonment was physical separation of the former couple plus an absence of consent to that separation on the part of the claimant. So you can still be 'abandoned' even if you know where your ex-partner is living.
3 This is according to Commissioner's decision CIS/1581/1998; in this case a woman and her daughter had left the matrimonial home because of her husband's violent behaviour, and had later returned to the home and claimed Income Support housing costs. The Commissioner held that she had been 'constructively abandoned' and should get help with her housing costs after the shorter waiting period.
Last updated September 2006

⇨ This information is part of a series of factsheets, produced by Gingerbread and kindly supported by HBOS. Reprinted with permission. Visit www.gingerbread.org.uk for more.
© Gingerbread

How many lone parents are receiving benefits?

Government paying tax credits and benefits to 200,000 more lone parents than live in the UK

The Government thinks it is paying out tax credits or out-of-work benefits to around 200,000 more lone parents than the Office for National Statistics estimate live in the UK, according to an analysis of official statistics by researchers at the IFS.

HM Revenue & Customs and the Department of Work and Pensions together estimate that they are paying income-related support for children to 2.1 million lone parents, even though the best estimate from other evidence is that there are only 1.9 million lone parents living in the UK.

Although there are other possibilities, it is highly likely that fraud or error explain much of this disparity. After analysing data from the latest Family Resources Survey (FRS), IFS researchers have concluded that a portion of the tax credits or out-of-work benefits which HMRC or DWP think they are paying to lone parents are probably being received by cohabiting couples with children, whether through deliberate fraud or errors made by claimants or the Government. If one disregards the threat of fines or penalties, it is often financially worthwhile to pretend to be a lone parent, rather than a couple, when claiming tax credits or out-of-work benefits.

'We already know that the tax credit system is subject to fraud from people using stolen identities. The latest figures provide powerful – albeit circumstantial – evidence that the system is also subject to fraud from families not being honest about their circumstances. Given the Government's reliance on tax credits to reduce child poverty, there is a need to review the safeguards against fraud in the tax credit system. To maintain political support for its policy of redistributing significantly more resources to less well-off families, the Government needs to be able to reassure taxpayers that their money is getting to those families that are genuinely entitled to it', says Mike Brewer, Programme Director of the Direct Tax and Welfare sector at the IFS.

> **Government departments estimate that they are paying income-related support for children to 2.1 million lone parents, even though there are only 1.9 million lone parents living in the UK**

Claims affected by fraud or error may also explain a small part of the gap between the £15 billion that the Government estimated that it paid to families with children in tax credits in 2004/05, and the £10 billion that was recorded by the FRS as being received by families. Instead, it is likely that much of this discrepancy arises because not all one-off payments of tax credits are captured in the FRS, and because adults are not always clear about which state benefits or tax credits they are receiving, perhaps because there have been so many changes to financial support for families with children since 1999. Whatever the reason, it seems that the FRS is producing an inaccurate impression of the incomes of families with children. Given that the Government is using tax credits as the main way to deliver support for families with children, and that it is committed to using the FRS to track child poverty to 2010/11, the Government should urgently review the quality of the data used to measure poverty.

12 March 2006

⇨ The above information is reprinted with kind permission from the Institute for Fiscal Studies. Visit www.ifs.org.uk for more information.

© *Institute for Fiscal Studies*

Top ten survival tips for lone parents

Information from One Parent Families

1. Make sure you are receiving all the financial support that you are entitled to

Splitting up from your partner may mean you become entitled to new benefits or tax credits or are now entitled to a higher amount. If you're already receiving benefit, or if your ex-partner was claiming benefits for the family, you must inform the benefits and/or tax credits office of the change. You should do this straight away so that you don't get overpaid or lose money. Call the Lone Parent Helpline on 0800 018 5026 for information about what you are entitled to.

> At times it can be difficult to cope as a lone parent, especially if you have just been through a bereavement or relationship breakdown

2. If you are unsure about your housing rights

After a relationship breakdown and/ or separation from your ex-partner, you will usually have the right to remain in your home. Contact Shelterline for free housing advice on 0808 800 4444 or call the Lone Parent helpline on 0800 018 5026 for help. You can also get advice from your local Citizens' Advice Bureau, the housing advice service at your local authority or a local law centre.

3. If you are experiencing violence or harassment

Women can contact the 24-hour National Domestic Violence free-phone helpline on 0808 2000 247 for

One parent families
making change happen

advice and information or if you need somewhere safe to stay. Men who are experiencing violence should call Mankind on 0870 794 4124 for support and referral to a refuge.

4. Make arrangements for child maintenance

Try to come to an agreement with your ex-partner. However, if this is not possible, contact the Child Support Agency national helpline on 08457 133 133, who can calculate and collect maintenance on your child's behalf. For more information read our *Making arrangements for child maintenance* factsheet. For a printed copy of the factsheet call the Lone Parent Helpline on 0800 018 5026.

5. Dealing with isolation and loneliness

At times it can be difficult to cope as a lone parent, especially if you have just been through a bereavement or relationship breakdown. Lots of lone parents find it helps to share experiences and ideas with people who have been through the same thing. Contact Gingerbread on 0800 018 4318 for details of support groups in your area. If you need some support and advice about parenting, contact Parentline Plus on 0808 800 2222.

6. Find out about childcare

Contact ChildcareLink on 0800 96 02 96 or see www.childcarelink.gov. uk for details of your local Children's Information Service (CIS) who can provide information about registered childcare providers in your area. If you are working, you can get help towards the costs of certain childcare through Working Tax Credit, call the Tax Credits Helpline on 0845 300 3900. If you are thinking of looking for work or training you may get help with childcare costs to do

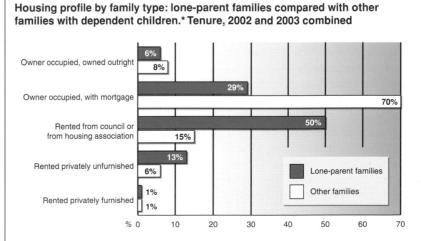

Housing and lone-parent families

Housing profile by family type: lone-parent families compared with other families with dependent children.* Tenure, 2002 and 2003 combined

Owner occupied, owned outright: 6% / 8%
Owner occupied, with mortgage: 29% / 70%
Rented from council or from housing association: 50% / 15%
Rented privately unfurnished: 13% / 6%
Rented privately furnished: 1% / 1%

■ Lone-parent families
□ Other families

*Dependent children are persons aged under 16, or aged 16-18 and in full-time education, in the family unit, and living in the household.

Source: Office for National Statistics. Crown copyright

this through the New Deal for Lone Parents, call the information line on 0800 868 868.

7. Ask your employer about flexible working

Find out if you have the right to ask your employer to consider a request for flexible working to change the hours and/or your patterns of work. You may also have the right to unpaid Parental leave. For more information call the Lone Parent Helpline on 0800 018 5026 and ask for our *Employment Rights* booklet.

8. Apply for a Council Tax discount

If you are the only adult in your household, you will qualify for a 25% discount on your Council Tax. Older children who you still receive Child Benefit for and students do not count as adults. Contact the Council Tax department at your local authority; the telephone number will be in your local directory.

Lots of lone parents find it helps to share experiences and ideas with people who have been through the same thing

---

9. Open your own bank account

If you have a joint bank account and/or credit card with your ex-partner, contact the bank to cancel it and open your own bank account. You will need this for any tax credit and/or benefit payments you are entitled to, as benefits are no longer paid by order book.

10. Make a Will

If you haven't already made a Will, you should do so now so that any property you own is distributed in the way you want and your wishes about your children are considered. You may also need to alter any Will you made before you separated from your ex-partner. For more information, call the Lone Parent

helpline on 0800 018 5026 and ask for the booklet, *Children's Rights and Parents' Responsibilities*.

⇨ The above information is reprinted with kind permission from One Parent Families, the charity promoting lone parents' welfare. To find out more about One Parent Families, please visit their website at www.oneparentfamilies.org.uk

© One Parent Families

Parenting alone

Information from TheSite.org

Being a single parent brings extra responsibilities. There are often financial pressures, which can make balancing demands at home and work a constant struggle.

At the same time, however, a lone parent can provide just as much respect and support to their children as any mum and dad put together. If not more. You may have double the workload. But not half the love.

If you're a single parent, here's how to make your family work as one:

⇨ Encourage your children to regard their family situation as normal. Stress that it doesn't take a mother and a father to make a whole.

⇨ Be open and honest with your children. Make them aware that you are there for any problems they may have and try not to hide your own. The stronger your channels of communication, the more confident your children will become.

⇨ Find appropriate role models for your child, preferably of the same sex as the absent parent.

⇨ Sort your legal situation, to be sure of your rights as the parent living with the child.

⇨ If you are separated or divorced from the other parent, try to make any visits arranged as pleasant as possible. Your child needs to feel loved and secure, whatever your relationship with his other parent.

⇨ Visits to or from the other parent should be as regular as possible. Plan ahead, but keep some flexibility on both sides.

⇨ Try not to treat visits as special occasions. Regard it as a chance to spend quality time together, but don't spoil the child. Often, doing everyday things together is of the most value to the child.

⇨ The above information is reprinted with kind permission from TheSite. org. For more information on this and other issues, please visit their website at www.thesite.org

© TheSite.org

Birth fathers' rights

Whether you're in a rock-steady relationship with the mother of your child, or barely on speaking terms, you have rights and responsibilities. Here's the deal

What does parental responsibility mean?

As the father of a child you have a duty to maintain the child until it leaves school by paying a proportion of your income. This can be done inside the relationship or, if it breaks up, either through agreement with the child's mother or through the Child Support Agency. This is your responsibility even if you weren't in a long-term relationship with the mother when the child was conceived.

If you are not married to the mother of your child, you won't have automatic parental responsibility – even if you are living with the child's mother.

Getting parental responsibility

You can get equal parental responsibility under any of the following circumstances:
- Registering the child's birth jointly with the child's mother;
- Making a parental responsibility agreement with the mother;
- Acquiring a parental responsibility order from a court;
- If you are appointed as guardian;
- If you marry the child's mother.

Legally, parental responsibility goes on until your child reaches 18 but as they get older so the law assumes that your child is more capable of making their own decisions.

What are the responsibilities?

As a parent (with parental responsibility) the Children Act 1989 says your responsibilities are 'all the rights, duties, powers, responsibilities and authority which by law a parent of a child has in relation to the child and his property'.

This includes:
- Safeguarding and promoting a child's health, development and welfare;
- Financially supporting the child;

TheSite.org

- Providing direction and guidance to the child;
- Maintaining direct and regular contact with the child;
- Acting as a legal representative until the child is 16 if required;
- Ensuring that the child is suitably educated.

In order to fulfil these responsibilities there are certain rights that can be used by the parent. These can include:
- Having the child living with the person with responsibility or having a say in where the child lives;
- Controlling, directing and guiding the child's upbringing;
- If the child is not living with you, having a personal relationship and regular contact with the child;
- Acting as a legal representative until the child is 16 if required;
- Choosing the child's name, but there may be restrictions on changing a child's name;
- Choosing the child's education;
- Being the person to give consent for medical treatment, issuing passports, adoption and marriage for a child under 18;
- Choosing a guardian for the child;
- Making decisions about the child's property on the child's behalf and for their benefit.

The child's mother wants to put the baby up for adoption
- Mothers can't give up the child for adoption until six weeks after its birth;

- Whether or not you are married to the mother you have automatic rights to be at the hearing;
- You no longer need a parental responsibility order to object to the adoption, as long as you and the mother register the birth of your baby together;
- You will be asked to give your consent for the adoption to go ahead, however, if you cannot be found then your consent is not needed;

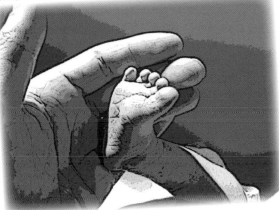

- If you do not consent the court has the power to override this refusal and still make an adoption order.

The law under review?

Child access laws may be amended in the near future, to enforce access arrangements where one parent refuses to comply. At present, many fathers complain that their ex-partners are ignoring any rulings or arrangments laid out by the courts. If the government review favours changes, this may mean parents who withhold access rights could be served a community service order, or even tagged.

- The above information is reprinted with kind permission from TheSite.org. Visit www.thesite.org for more information.

© TheSite.org

KEY FACTS

⇨ One in five young men and nearly half of young women aged 16-24 said they wished they had waited longer to start having sex. They were twice as likely to say this if they had been under 15 when they first had sex. (page 1)

⇨ The UK has the highest teenage birth and abortion rates in Western Europe. (page 2)

⇨ In the 1970s, Britain had similar teenage pregnancy rates to the rest of Europe. But while other countries got theirs down in the 1980s and 1990s, Britain's rate stayed high. (page 4)

⇨ Groups who are more vulnerable to becoming teenage parents include young people who are: in or leaving care, homeless, underachieving at school, children of teenage parents, members of some ethnic groups, involved in crime, living in areas with higher social deprivation. (page 5)

⇨ Pregnancy (conception) occurs when a sperm fertilises an egg by joining with it during sex. This can happen when two people have sex and do not use contraception. A fertilised egg will then move down into a girl's uterus and implant itself into the womb (uterus) lining where it will begin to grow. (page 8)

⇨ Children of teenage mothers suffer as young adults in terms of lower educational attainment, a higher risk of economic inactivity and of becoming a teenage mother themselves. This may result because of the lower standard of living experienced by many teenage mothers, owing in part to the poorer earning partners that they pair with. (page 10)

⇨ 42% of children were born outside marriage in the UK in 2004, compared with only 12% in 1980. (page 11)

⇨ 83 per cent of parents of school-age children think that schools should teach young people about the emotional aspects of sex and relationships as well as the biological facts, according to a new survey. (page 16)

⇨ Children should be taught about the importance of contraception in their last year of primary school, according to new research from the Institute for Public Policy Research. (page 17)

⇨ 38% of 15-year-olds in the UK had sex in the period 2001/02. (page 17)

⇨ Only 49 per cent of respondents to a YWCA survey think teenage mums are responsible (compared to 91 per cent for mums in general). (page 18)

⇨ Many teenagers interviewed by the Joseph Rowntree Foundation cited motherhood as a better option than the prospect of a low-paid, dead-end job. Some saw parenthood as an opportunity to change their life, gain independence and create a new identity – all within their own control. (page 20)

⇨ Research shows that underachievers are more likely to become teenage parents. Their children are also likely to continue the pattern of underachievement. (page 24)

⇨ According to research, if a father is present at the birth, and has his name on the birth certificate, the chances of remaining positively in the baby's life are vastly increased. (page 26)

⇨ Schoolgirls at risk of pregnancy could be sent on a programme that uses babies to put them off premature parenthood, under new government plans to tackle teenage conception. (page 27)

⇨ There are 1.8 million one-parent families in Britain and they care for nearly 3 million children. About nine out of ten lone parents are women. The median age for a lone parent is 35, and at any one time only 3 per cent of lone mothers are teenagers. (page 28)

⇨ 66% of dependent children live with a married couple. 11% live with a cohabiting couple, 22% with a lone mother, and 2% with a lone father. (page 29)

⇨ Between 2003 and 2004, the percentage of lone-parent households (with one child) was ten times less likely to be on the £500-£600 (a week) income bracket than a two-parent household with one child. (page 30)

⇨ A study by Dr Libertad Gonzalez of the Pompeu Fabra University in Barcelona found that eight per cent of British women aged between 18 and 35 are bringing up children on their own. (page 32)

⇨ The Government thinks it is paying out tax credits or out-of-work benefits to around 200,000 more lone parents than the Office for National Statistics estimate live in the UK, according to an analysis of official statistics by researchers at the IFS. (page 36)

⇨ 50% of lone-parent families live in a home rented from a council or housing association. (page 37)

⇨ The father of a child has a duty to maintain the child until it leaves school by paying a proportion of his income. This is the father's responsibility even if he wasn't in a long-term relationship with the mother when the child was conceived. (page 39)

GLOSSARY

Abortion
The artificial ending of a pregnancy before it has reached full term. In England, Wales and Scotland, the law says this must take place before the 24th week of pregnancy. Of the 97,107 pregnancies which occurred in girls aged under 20 in England and Wales in 2001, 58,340 ended in abortion, while 38,767 ended in maternity.

Age of consent
The age at which an individual can legally take part in sexual intercourse. In England and Wales, the age of consent to any form of sexual activity is 16 for both men and women, whether they are heterosexual, homosexual or bisexual. In Scotland, the age of consent for women and for sex between men is 16. In Northern Ireland, the age of consent for women and for sex between men is 17.

Benefits
Benefits available to lone parents include Child Tax Credit, Income Support, Jobseeker's Allowance, Child Maintenance, Housing Benefit and Working Tax Credit. What a parent can claim depends on their individual circumstances. Some people claim that the UK, which has one of the highest levels of state benefits for single parents in Europe, is encouraging people to bring up their children alone.

Contraception
Contraception is used during sexual intercourse to prevent pregnancy. Barrier methods such as condoms are also effective in preventing sexually transmitted infections. The most common types of contraception are condoms and 'the pill' (the combined or mini contraceptive pill). Emergency contraception such as the 'morning-after pill' can also be used for a limited period after sex to prevent a pregnancy.

Dependent children
A dependent child is one who is still reliant on their parent or parents to meet their basic needs. The government defines this as any child in a household who is under 16, or aged 16-18, in full-time education and never married.

Lone-parent family
Also called one-parent or single-parent families. A lone parent can be male or female, but nine out of ten lone parents are women who are raising children without a partner after divorce, separation, death, abandonment or other reason. Contrary to popular public opinion, only 3% of lone parents in Britain are teenage mothers.

Sex education
Sex education takes place in schools; its purpose is to help young people acquire information and form attitudes about sex, sexual identity, relationships and intimacy, so that they can make informed decisions about their own sexual activities and avoid unwanted outcomes such as unplanned pregnancy or infection with sexually transmitted diseases. Currently it is only compulsory for schools to teach the biological aspects of sex; however, there have been calls for a wider-ranging form of sex education, including teaching on relationships, to be made compulsory.

INDEX

Additional Resources

Other Issues titles

If you are interested in researching further some of the issues raised in *Teen Pregnancy and Lone Parents*, you may like to read the following titles in the **Issues** series:

⇨ Vol. 126 *The Abortion Debate* (ISBN 978 1 86168 365 6)

⇨ Vol. 124 *Parenting Issues* (ISBN 978 1 86168 363 2)

⇨ Vol. 123 *Young People and Health* (ISBN 978 1 86168 362 5)

⇨ Vol. 112 *Women, Men and Equality* (ISBN 978 1 86168 345 8)

⇨ Vol. 110 *Poverty* (ISBN 978 1 86168 343 4)

⇨ Vol. 106 *Trends in Marriage* (ISBN 978 1 86168 326 7)

⇨ Vol. 96 *Preventing Sexual Diseases* (ISBN 978 1 86168 304 5)

⇨ Vol. 74 *Money Matters* (ISBN 978 1 86168 263 5)

⇨ Vol. 20 *Population Growth* (ISBN 978 1 86168 166 9)

For more information about these titles, visit our website at www.independence.co.uk/publicationslist

Useful organisations

You may find the websites of the following organisations useful for further research:

⇨ AVERT: www.avert.org

⇨ Basic Skills Agency: www.basic-skills.co.uk

⇨ Citizens' Advice Bureau: www.citizensadvice.org.uk

⇨ Civitas: www.civitas.org.uk

⇨ Department for Education and Skills: www.dfes.gov.uk

⇨ Economic and Social Research Council: www.esrc.ac.uk

⇨ **fpa**: www.fpa.org.uk

⇨ Gingerbread: www.gingerbread.org.uk

⇨ Institute for Fiscal Studies: www.ifs.org.uk

⇨ Institute for Public Policy Research: www.ippr.org.uk

⇨ Joseph Rowntree Foundation: www.jrf.org.uk

⇨ Marie Stopes International: www.likeitis.org

⇨ NCB's Sex Education Forum: www.ncb.org.uk/sef

⇨ Office for National Statistics: www.statistics.gov.uk

⇨ One Parent Families: www.oneparentfamilies.org.uk

⇨ Teenage Pregnancy Unit: www..dfes.gov.uk/teenagepregnancy

⇨ TheSite: www.thesite.org

⇨ YWCA: www.ywca-gb.org.uk

ACKNOWLEDGEMENTS

The publisher is grateful for permission to reproduce the following material.

While every care has been taken to trace and acknowledge copyright, the publisher tenders its apology for any accidental infringement or where copyright has proved untraceable. The publisher would be pleased to come to a suitable arrangement in any such case with the rightful owner.

Chapter One: Teenage Parents

Teenagers: sexual health and behaviour, © fpa, *Information on teenage pregnancy*, © Crown copyright is reproduced with the permission of Her Majesty's Stationery Office, *Teenage pregnancy*, © fpa, *Teenage pregnancy – what to do*, © Marie Stopes International, *Consequences of teenage births*, © Crown copyright is reproduced with the permission of Her Majesty's Stationery Office, *Sex education and teenage pregnancy*, © Crown copyright is reproduced with the permission of Her Majesty's Stationery Office, *Sex education that works*, © AVERT, *Beyond biology*, © NCB, *Call for sex education in primary schools*, © ippr, *Mum's the word*, © YWCA, *Pregnancy in teenage girls 'all part of nature's law'*, © Scotsman Publications Ltd, *Poverty and young parenthood*, © Joseph Rowntree Foundation, *Teenage mums should not be stigmatised*, © YWCA, *The stigma of being a teenage mum*, © Guardian Newspapers Ltd 2006, *Getting teenage mums 'back to school'*, © Basic Skills Agency, *When lads become dads*, © Guardian Newspapers Ltd 2006, *Toddlers to help halt teen pregnancies*, © Guardian Newspapers Ltd 2006.

Chapter Two: Lone-Parent Families

Welfare and single parenthood in the UK, © ESRC, *Lone-parent families*, © Gingerbread, *Dependent children*, © Crown copyright is reproduced with the permission of Her Majesty's Stationery Office, *Why UK is Europe's single-parent capital*, © 2006 Associated Newspapers Ltd, *Benefits and tax credits*, © Gingerbread, *How many lone parents are receiving benefits?*, © Institute for Fiscal Studies, *Top ten survival tips for lone parents*, © One Parent Families, *Parenting alone*, © TheSite.org, *Birth fathers' rights*, © TheSite.org.

Photographs and illustrations:

Pages 1, 5, 25, 36: Don Hatcher; pages 6, 14, 22, 27: Angelo Madrid; pages 10, 21, 24, 38: Simon Kneebone; pages 12, 23: Bev Aisbett.

And with thanks to the team: Mary Chapman, Sandra Dennis and Jan Haskell.

Lisa Firth
Cambridge
January, 2007